Street by Street

# WIGAN

## ASHTON-IN-MAKERFIELD, LEIGH, SKELMERSDALE

### Abram, Aspull, Atherton, Billinge, Golborne, Hindley, Ince-in-Makerfield, Orrell, Rainford, Standish, Tyldesley, Westhoughton





Ist edition May 2002



Published by AA Publishing (a trading name of Automobile Association Developments Limited, whose registered office is Millstream, Maidenhead Road, Windsor, Berkshire SL4 5GD. Registered number 1878835).



Schools address data provided by Education Direct.

Mapping produced by the Cartographic Department of The Automobile Association. A00965

A CIP Catalogue record for this book is available from the British Library.

Printed by GRAFIASA S.A., Porto Portugal.



Ref: ML201

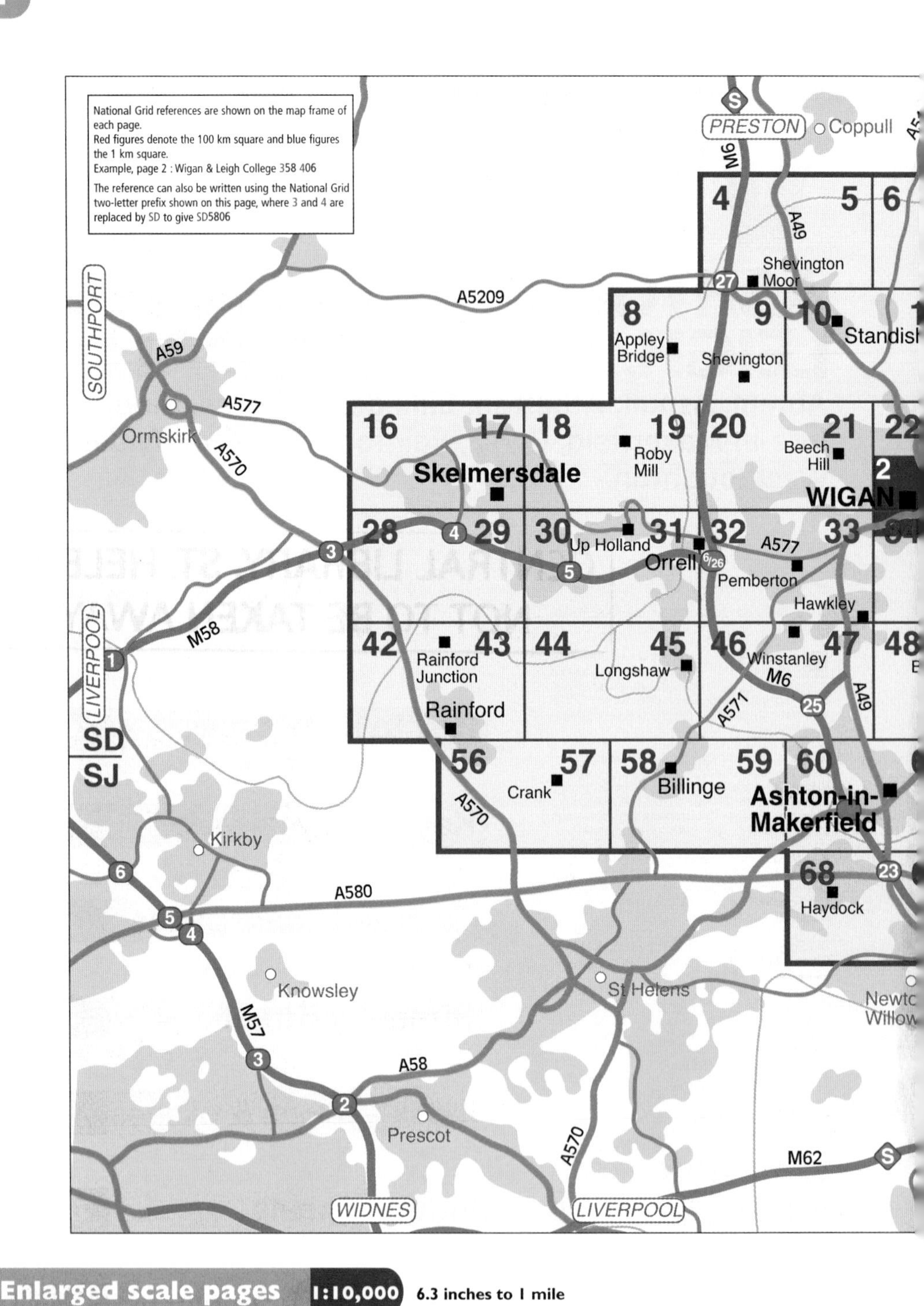

National Grid references are shown on the map frame of each page.
Red figures denote the 100 km square and blue figures the 1 km square.
Example, page 2 : Wigan & Leigh College 358 406
The reference can also be written using the National Grid two-letter prefix shown on this page, where 3 and 4 are replaced by SD to give SD5806
PRESTON
Coppull
M6
A49
4
5
6
Shevington Moor
27
A5209
8
9
10
Appley Bridge
Shevington
Standish
SOUTHPORT
A59
A577
Ormskirk
A570
16
17
18
19
20
21
22
Skelmersdale
Roby Mill
Beech Hill
2
WIGAN
28
29
30
31
32
33
4
3
5
Up Holland
Orrell
6/26
A577
Pemberton
Hawkley
LIVERPOOL
1
M58
42
43
44
45
46
47
48
Rainford Junction
Longshaw
Winstanley
M6
A571
25
A49
Rainford
SD
SJ
56
57
58
59
60
Crank
Billinge
Ashton-in-Makerfield
A570
Kirkby
68
23
Haydock
6
A580
5
4
Knowsley
St Helens
M57
3
A58
2
Prescot
A570
M62
S
WIDNES
LIVERPOOL

## Enlarged scale pages 1:10,000

6.3 inches to 1 mile

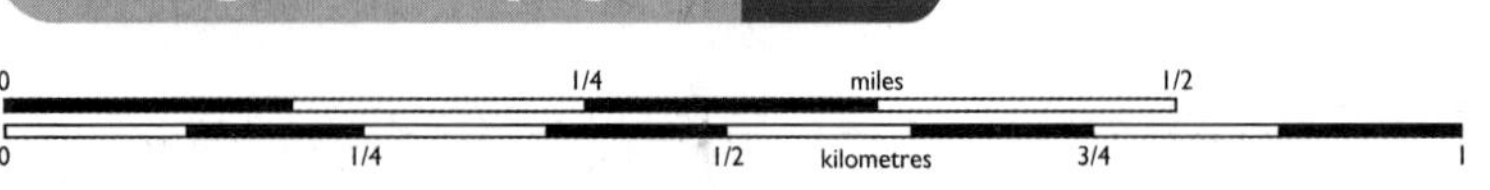

0
1/4
miles
1/2
0
1/4
1/2
kilometres
3/4
1

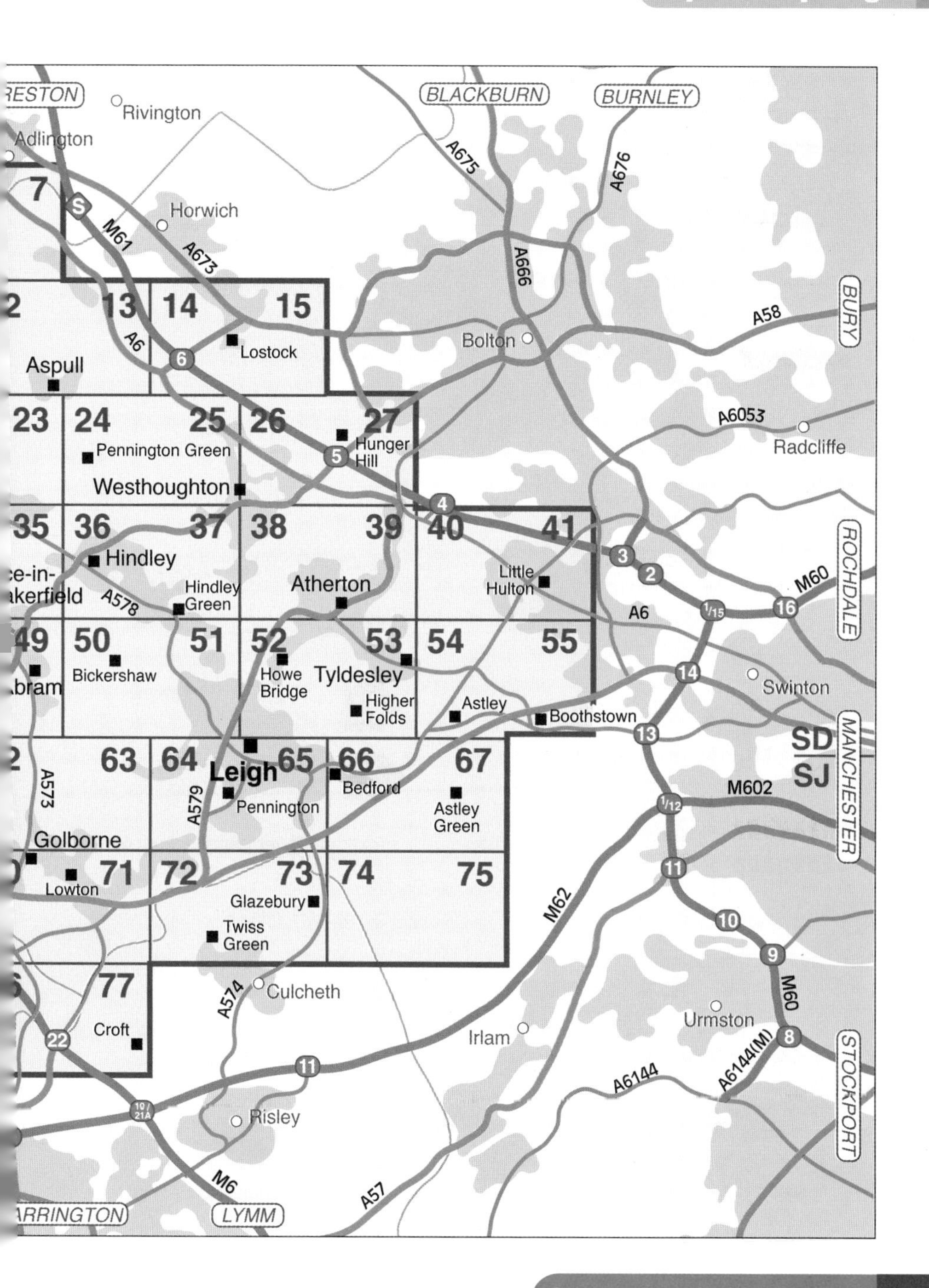


4.2 inches to 1 mile

**Scale of main map pages 1:15,000**

0 | 1/4 | miles | 1/2 | 3/4 | 1

0 | 1/4 | 1/2 | kilometres 3/4 | 1 | 1 1/4 | 1 1/2

Junction 9 Motorway & junction

Services Motorway service area

Primary road single/dual carriageway

Services Primary road service area

A road single/dual carriageway

B road single/dual carriageway

Other road single/dual carriageway

Minor/private road, access may be restricted

One-way street

Pedestrian area

Track or footpath

Road under construction

Road tunnel

AA AA Service Centre

P Parking

P+ Park & Ride

Bus/Coach station

Railway & main railway station

Railway & minor railway station

Underground station

Light Railway & station

Preserved private railway

LC Level crossing

Tramway

Ferry route

Airport runway

Boundaries - borough/district

Mounds

93 Page continuation 1:15,000

7 Page continuation to enlarged scale 1:10,000

River/canal, lake, pier

Aqueduct, lock, weir

465 Winter Hill Peak (with height in metres)

Beach

Coniferous woodland

Broadleaved woodland

Mixed woodland

Park

| | |
|---|---|
| | Cemetery |
| | Built-up area |
| | Featured building |
| | City wall |
| A&E | 24-hour Accident & Emergency hospital |
| PO | Post Office |
| | Public library |
| i | Tourist Information Centre |
| | Petrol station<br>Major suppliers only |
| | Church/chapel |
| | Toilet |
| | Toilet with disabled facilities |
| PH | Public house<br>AA recommended |
| | Restaurant<br>AA inspected |
| | Theatre or performing arts centre |
| | Cinema |
| | Golf course |
| | Camping<br>AA inspected |
| | Caravan Site<br>AA inspected |
| | Camping & Caravan Site<br>AA inspected |

| | |
|---|---|
| | Theme Park |
| | Abbey, cathedral or priory |
| | Castle |
| | Historic house or building |
| Wakehurst Place NT | National Trust property |
| M | Museum or art gallery |
| | Roman antiquity |
| | Ancient site, battlefield or monument |
| | Industrial interest |
| | Garden |
| | Arboretum |
| | Farm or animal centre |
| | Zoological or wildlife collection |
| | Bird collection |
| | Nature reserve |
| V | Visitor or heritage centre |
| | Country park |
| | Cave |
| | Windmill |
| | Distillery, brewery or vineyard |

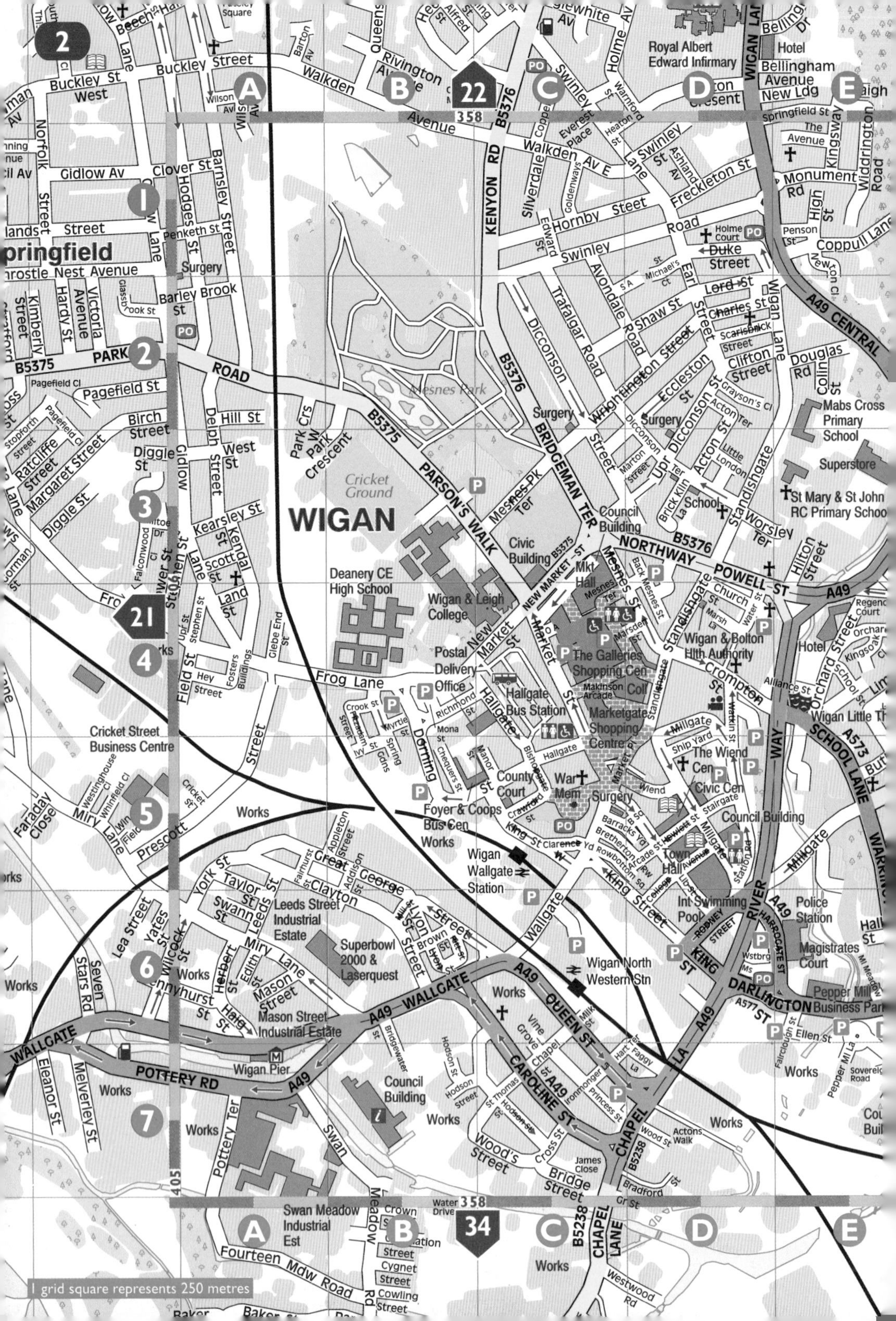

2
22
21
34
A
B
C
D
E
1
3
4
5
6
7
358
405
WIGAN
Springfield
Royal Albert Edward Infirmary
Hotel
Bellingham Avenue
New Ldg
Springfield St
The Avenue
Kingsway
Widdrington Road
Monument Rd
High St
Penson St
Coppull Lane
Newton Cl
A49 CENTRAL
Buckley Street
Buckley St West
Norfolk Street
Gidlow Av
Clover St
Hodges St
Barnsley Street
Penketh St
Gidlow Lane
Throstle Nest Avenue
Kimberly Street
Hardy St
Victoria Avenue
Surgery
Barley Brook St
PO
B5375
PARK ROAD
Pagefield Cl
Pagefield St
Birch Street
Hill St
Delph Street
West St
Diggle St
Stopforth Street
Ratcliffe Street
Margaret Street
Kearsley St
Kendal St
Scott St
Land St
Stephen St
Hey Street
Fosters Buildings
Glebe End St
Field St
Walkden Avenue
Rivington Avenue
Queens
Barton Av
Alfred St
KENYON RD
B5376
Silverdale
Coppe
Everest Place
Walkden Av E
Heaton St
Warnford St
Holme Av
Swinley Lane
Swinley St
Ashland Av
Freckleton St
Hornby Street
Edward St
Swinley Road
Holme Court
Duke Street
Lord St
Charles St
Scarisbrick Street
Clifton Street
Douglas Rd
Collin St
Mabs Cross Primary School
Superstore
St Mary & St John RC Primary School
Avondale Road
Trafalgar Road
Dicconson Street
Shaw St
Wrightington Street
Eccleston St
Grayson's Cl
Acton St
Acton Ter
Little London
Standishgate
Worsley Ter
Hilton Street
Mesnes Park
Park Crs W
Park Crescent
Cricket Ground
PARSON'S WALK
BRIDGEMAN TER
Mesnes Pk Ter
Council Building
Civic Building
NORTHWAY
POWELL ST
A49
Regent Court
Orchard Street
Kingsoak
Deanery CE High School
Wigan & Leigh College
NEW MARKET ST
Mkt Hall
Mesnes St
Back Mesnes St
Church St
Marsh La
Water St
Wigan & Bolton Hlth Authority
Hotel
Alliance St
Wigan Little Th
SCHOOL LANE
A573
Postal Delivery Office
Frog Lane
New Market St
Market St
The Galleries Shopping Cen
Makinson Arcade
Marketgate Shopping Centre
Crompton St
Millgate
Ship Yard
The Wiend
Civic Cen
Crook St
Myrtle St
Richmond St
Mona St
Hallgate
Hallgate Bus Station
Dorning St
Chequers St
Manor St
County Court
Bishopgate
War Mem
Crawford St
Foyer & Coops Bus Cen
Stairgate
Council Building
Cricket Street Business Centre
Westinghouse Cl
Whinfield Cl
Miry Lane
Prescott Street
Faraday Close
Works
Wigan Wallgate Station
King St
Clarence Yd
Barracks Yd
Bretherton Rw
Rowbottom Sq
Arcade St
Hewlett St
College Av
Town Hall
Library St
Station Rd
King Street
Wallgate
Int Swimming Pool
RODNEY STREET
KING ST
RIVER WAY
HARROGATE ST
Police Station
Magistrates Court
Wstbrg Ms
DARLINGTON ST
A577
Ellen St
Pepper Mill Business Park
Pepper Mi La
Sovereign Road
Appleton Street
Great George Street
Addison St
Clayton St
Fairhurst St
Leeds Street Industrial Estate
Superbowl 2000 & Laserquest
York St
Taylor St
Swann St
Leeds St
Lyon St
Brown St
Lea Street
Yates St
Wilcock St
Herbert St
Edith St
Mason Street
Mason Street Industrial Estate
Haig St
Seven Stars Rd
A49 WALLGATE
Wigan North Western Stn
QUEEN ST
CAROLINE ST
Vine Grove
Chapel St
Hart St
Faggy La
Ironmonger La
Princess St
POTTERY RD
Wigan Pier
Eleanor St
Melverley St
Pottery Ter
Bridgewater St
Hodson St
Council Building
St Thomas St
Wood's Street
Cross St
James Close
Bridge Street
CHAPEL LA
B5238
Wood St
Actons Walk
Bradford St
Swan Meadow Industrial Est
Meadow Rd
Crown St
Water Drive
CHAPEL LANE
Fourteen Mdw Road
Street
Cygnet Street
Cowling Street
Westwood Rd
Baker
1 grid square represents 250 metres

F
G
H
22
J
K
59
60
Rosemary Crs
Chestnut Road
Cedar Drive
Chestnut Road
Avenue
Balniel Walk
Whelley
Plantation Gates
Balcarres
Walnut Av
St Stephens Primary School
Whelley Hospital
Bradshaw Street
Fellside
West Mount
Moore St
Pyke St
Hieland Rd
Nutt St
Newman St
Salcombe Cl
WHELLEY
Elworthy Grove
St Stephen's Av
Round House Av
Durham Street
Nottingham Pl
Highfield Av
Berwick Pl
Lamb St
Wallace La
Weldon Grove
Moore St E
Salmon Street
Palewood Cl
Malpas Av
School Av
Thompson St
Ellis St
Eckersley St
Wright St
Sedwyn St
Kelway Ter
Alwyn St
Alwyn Ter
Vine St
Great Acre
Wynard Av
Riverside Av
Rowanhill
WN1
B5238
Northumberland Street
Sole St
Roach Gn
Perch St
Westmoorland St
Durham St
Bedford Street
Windermere St
Essex St
Longshoot Close
Coop St
Longshoot Health Centre
Bolton Square
Oxford Court
Riley Sq
Longshoot
Molyneux St
Sullivan Wy
Platt Lane
Knowles Place
Stanley Place
Golborne Place
Kendrick Place
Wells Place
Caunce Rd
Caunce Road
Isabella Square
Quarry Place
Kirklees St
Linney Square
Kirklees Street
Florence St
Scholes
SCHOLES
Scholes Shopping Pecinct
Baldwin St
Bryham St
Gilroy St
Belvoir St
Vauxhall Rd
Scholefield Lane
Caunce St
Catherine Ter
Lorne St
Cecil St
Church Grove
Leader St
Birkett St
Frederic St
Kirklees St
St Catherines CE Primary School
Collett Cl
Hackworth Cl
Gresley Cl
Hardybutts
Edwin St
Birkett Bank
Bradshawgate
John St
St Patricks Wy
Junior School
Patrick St
Fowler Cl
Rupert St
Primary School
Hunt St
Roscoe St
Oak St
Vulcan Dr
A577
DARLINGTON STREET EAST
Chatham St
Harper St
Inglewood Av
Hartley Av
Ascroft St
Cambridge St
Clarington Grove
Henry Pk St
Gordon St
Spring Gv
Spring St
Leigh St
Kent St
Shared
Boundary Street
Spring View Cricket Club
Works
Whelley
Ross Close
Stroud Close
Cheltenham St
Tamworth Dr
Stanstead Close
Albury
Wells Drive
Hilton Avenue
Burnham Grove
Ashbourne Av
Alston Road
Milford Road
Shildon Close
Borden Close
Horsham Grove
Maldon Close
Grantham Grove
Bamford Drive
Amberley Close
Camberwell
Crescent
Camberwell Crescent
Finchley Crs
Corsock Drive
Dalbeatie Rise
Bengairn Close
Waterbeck Close
Tinwald Place
Lea View
Lyefield Av
Woodchurch
Northcroft
Farnsfield
Swinside
Gillbrow Crs
Baclaw Close
Trecastell Cl
Leybourn Cl
Rose Bridge High School
Street
Georges La
Waters Reach
Locks View
Holt
Edward St
Karen Rd
Brock St
Wray St
Caroline St
Moorings Cl
MANCHESTER ROAD
Markland St
Rosebridge Wy
Rose St
Street
Forge St
Broomfield Terrace
Broomfield Ter
Canal Terrace
Empress Industrial Estate
Hall Avenue
Ince Hall St
Works
Clegg St
Keble St
Stopford St
Smithy Green
Surgery
School St
Hook St
Local Board St
Leaway
Pryce Av
The Grove
Greenfield
Kingsway
Loeminster Place
Meadway
Anderton Av
Amar St
Bird
Ince Green
Heber St
George Street
St Williams RC School
Ince CE Primary School
Ince-In-Makerfield
34
Ince Gn La
Patricroft Rd
Pinewood Crs
Maple Av
Canal Street
Ince Green Lane
Redbrook Road
Baverstock Cl
Kellaton Cl
Primary School
Pitt St
Lancaster
Richard
RC Primary School
Silvington Way
Marchbank
Dryton Walk
Avenue
Montford Rise
Ashbourne Av
Holmsfield
Bromley Close
I
2
3
Leeds Liverpool Canal
23
Rathen Av
Turriff Gv
Falkirk
West
Chatham
Stirling Av
Perth Av
Pennington La
Belle Green Industrial Estate
Gidlow St
Reservoir St
4
5
6
7
Careless Lane
County
Police St
Jeffrey St
Queensway
Engineer St
Humphrey
Earl St
Ince Clinic &
Brook St
Belle Gn La
Union St
King St
Works
Pinfold St
Darlington Street
Lord St
Ellen St
Charles St
Pickup St
Jackson St
Branch St
Brown St
Infant School
Dobson Pkwy
Mitchell St
WN2
405
Dobson Park Industrial Estate
Parkway
Dobson
Works

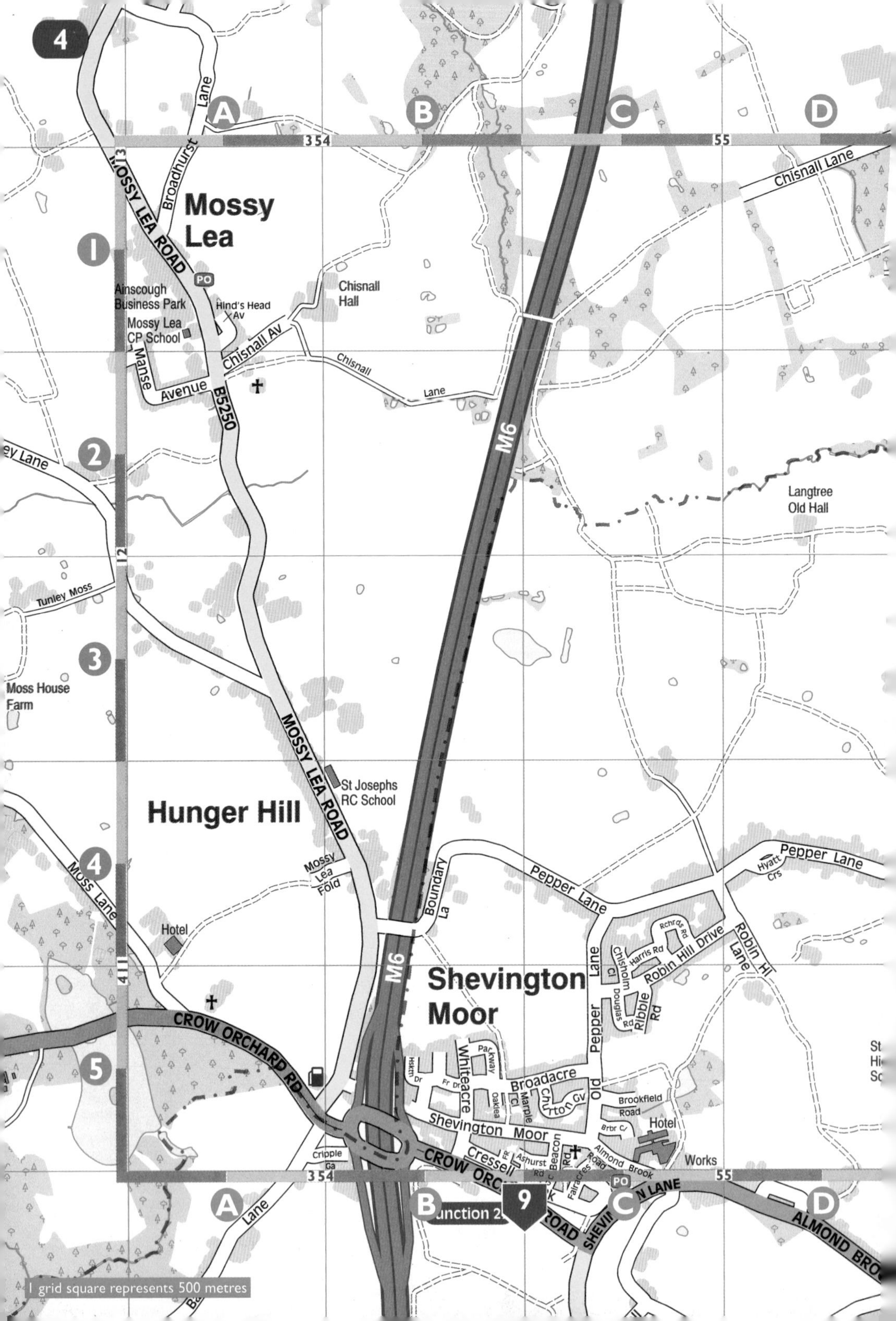

A
B
C
D
354
55
1
2
3
4
5
13
12
411
Mossy Lea
MOSSY LEA ROAD
Broadhurst Lane
PO
Ainscough Business Park
Hind's Head Av
Mossy Lea CP School
Manse Avenue
Chisnall Av
Chisnall Lane
B5250
Chisnall Hall
Chisnall Lane
M6
Langtree Old Hall
Tunley Moss
Moss House Farm
St Josephs RC School
Hunger Hill
Mossy Lea Fold
Moss Lane
Hotel
Boundary La
Pepper Lane
Hyatt Crs
Robin Hill Drive
Robin Hill Lane
Harris Rd
Chisholm Cl
Douglas Rd
Ribble Rd
Shevington Moor
Pepper Lane
Old
CROW ORCHARD RD
Parkway
Whiteacre
Broadacre
Churton Gv
Brookfield Road
Oaklea Cl
Marple
Shevington Moor
Hotel
Cressell
Ashurst Rd
Beacon
Almond Brook Road
Fairacres
Works
Cripple Ga
CROW ORCHARD ROAD
SHEVINGTON LANE
ALMOND BROOK
Junction 27
9
Lane
1 grid square represents 500 metres

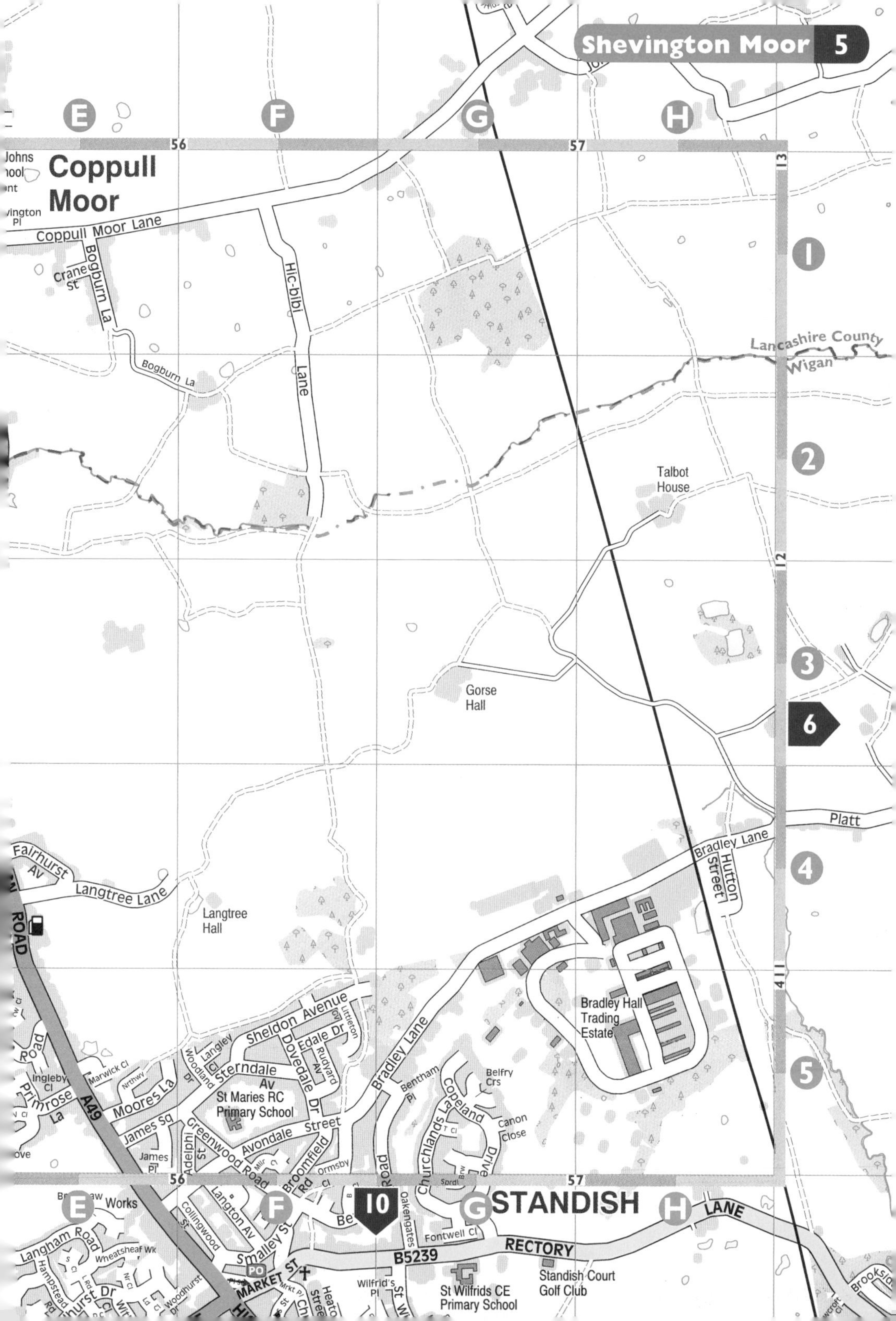
Coppull Moor
Coppull Moor Lane
Bogburn La
Crane St
Hic-bibi Lane
Lancashire County
Wigan
Talbot House
Gorse Hall
Platt
Bradley Lane
Hutton Street
Fairhurst Av
Langtree Lane
Langtree Hall
Bradley Hall Trading Estate
Sheldon Avenue
Edale Dr
Dovedale Dr
Rudyard Av
Littleton Gv
Sterndale Av
Woodland Dr
Langley Cl
Marwick Cl
Ingleby Cl
Primrose La
Moores La
St Maries RC Primary School
James Sq
Adelphi St
Greenwood Road
Avondale Street
Broomfield Rd
Ormsby Cl
Bentham Pl
Copeland Drive
Churchlands La
Belfry Crs
Canon Close
A49
ROAD
STANDISH
Works
Langham Road
Langton Av
Collingwood St
Smalley St
Oakengates
Fontwell Cl
RECTORY LANE
B5239
MARKET ST
Wilfrid's Pl
St Wilfrids CE Primary School
Standish Court Golf Club
Wheatsheaf Wk
PO
10
6
E F G H
1 2 3 4 5
56 57
13 12 411

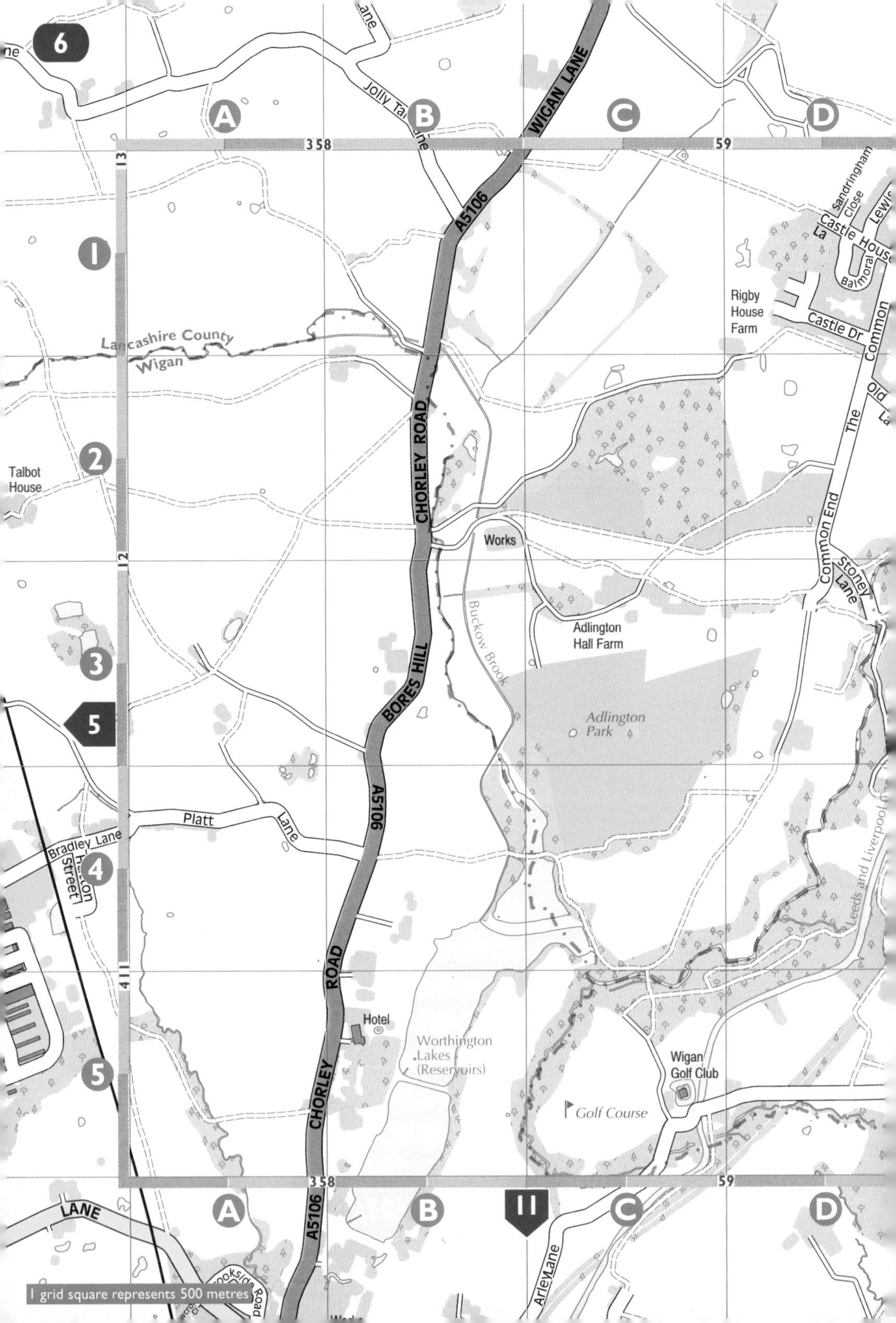
6
Jolly Tar Lane
WIGAN LANE
A
B
C
D
358
59
13
1
2
3
4
5
12
411
A5106
CHORLEY ROAD
BORES HILL
Lancashire County
Wigan
Talbot House
Sandringham Close
Castle House La
Balmoral
Lewis
Rigby House Farm
Castle Dr
Common
The Old La
The Common End
Stoney Lane
Works
Buckow Brook
Adlington Hall Farm
Adlington Park
Platt Lane
Bradley Lane
Hilton Street
Leeds and Liverpool Canal
Hotel
Worthington Lakes (Reservoirs)
Wigan Golf Club
Golf Course
LANE
11
Arley Lane
Brookside Road
1 grid square represents 500 metres

ADLINGTON
Blackrod
Little Scotland
Adlington CP School
Adlington Station
Adlington Cricket Club
Works
Cemetery
Gas St
Grove Avenue
Railway Road
Church St
Market Place
Market St
Chorley Road
A6
A673
Bolton Road
M61
Grimeford Industrial Estate
Grimeford Lane
Greenland
Huyton Road
Meadow Street
Belmont Road
Abbey Gv
Mayfield Av
Anglezarke Rd
Shawes
Back Railway View
Station Rd
Water St
Oxford St
Harrison Road
Outterside Street
The Poplars
Chapel St
Grafton St
Marlow Ct
Warwick St
Blackrod Brow
Dark Lane
Aberdeen Farm
Crowshaw Farm
Blundell Lane
Arley Lane
Scotland Lane
Little Scotland
Tucker's
Sibberings Farm
Half Acre Lane
Nightingale Rd
Thirlmere Rd
Harrison Crs
Ainse Road
Clifton Dr
Hill Lane
Vicarage Rd W
Ridgway
Surgery
Council Building
Blackrod Church School
Black Horse St
Church Street
Folds
Coniston Road
Whitehall Lane
Carlton Close
Fryent Close
Brown St
Vicarage Road
Lymbridge Drive
Greenbank
Vauze Av
Grove
Calderas Lane
Bolton Wigan
60
61
12
E
F
G
H
1
2
3
4
5
PO

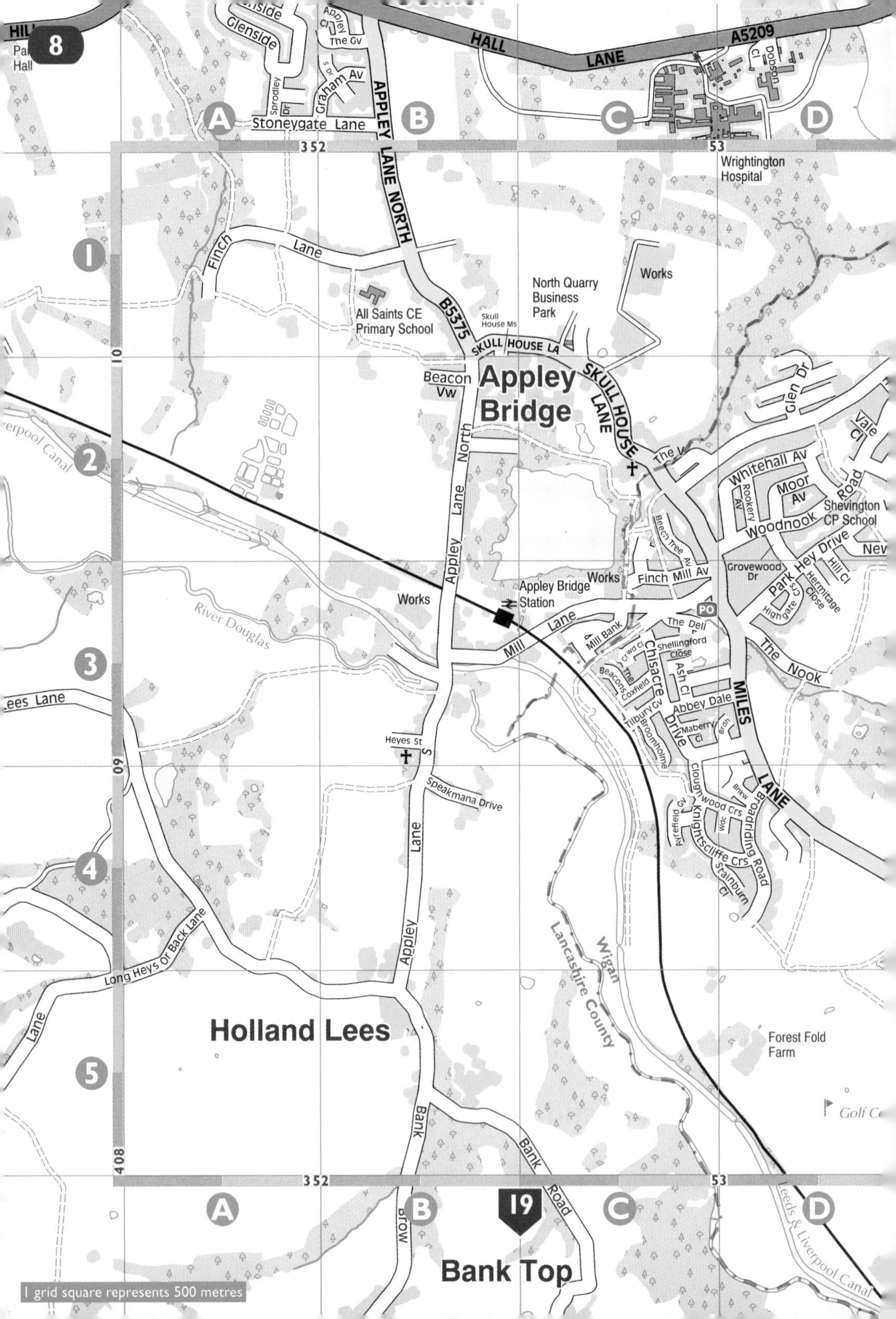
8
Park Hall
Glenside
Appley Cl
The Gv
S Dr
Graham Av
Sprodley Dr
Stoneygate Lane
HALL LANE
A5209
Dobson Cl
APPLEY LANE NORTH
Wrightington Hospital
Finch Lane
Works
North Quarry Business Park
All Saints CE Primary School
B5375
Skull House Ms
SKULL HOUSE LA
SKULL HOUSE LANE
Beacon Vw
Appley Bridge
Glen Dr
Vale Cl
The V
Whitehall Av
Moor Av
Rookery Av
Woodnook Road
Shevington CP School
Beech Tree Av
Park Hey Drive
Hill Cl
Grovewood Dr
Hermitage Close
Highgate Crs
Finch Mill Av
Appley Lane North
Liverpool Canal
River Douglas
Appley Bridge Station
Mill Lane
PO
The Dell
Mill Bank
Shellingford Close
Crwd Cl
The Beacons
Coxfield
Chisacre Drive
Ash Cl
Abbey Dale
Tilbury Gv
Maberry Cl
Broomholme
Brdh
MILES LANE
The Nook
Lees Lane
Heyes St
Speakmana Drive
Cloughwood Crs
Knightscliffe Crs
Ayrefield Gv
Wdc
Bnkw
Broadriding Road
Stainburn Cl
Appley Lane
Long Heys Or Back Lane
Lane
Lancashire County
Wigan
Holland Lees
Forest Fold Farm
Golf C
Bank
Bank Road
Brow
Bank Top
Leeds & Liverpool Canal
A B C D
1 2 3 4 5
352
53
10
09
408
19
1 grid square represents 500 metres

Shevington Vale
Shevington
WN6
Junction 27
CROW ORCHARD ROAD
SHEVINGTON LANE
ALMOND BROOK ROAD
A5209
Back Lane
Cripple
Shevington
Cressell Pk
Broadacre
Whiteacre
Parkway
Oaklea
Churton Gv
Old
Brookfield Road
Hotel
Beacon Rd
Fairacres
Almond Brook Road
Works
Aspinall Rd
Arbour Lane
Primrose La
Foxglove Cl
Bradshaw Cl
Langham Road
Cranborn Cl
Hampstead Rd
Woodhurst
Spey Cl
Cemetery
Paradise Farm
Shevington County High School
Parbrook Lane
Park Av
Kilburn Dr
Copperas Cl
Lyndon Av
Orch Cl
Willowbrook Dr
Park Field
Longbrook
Yewdale
High Park
Millbrook CP Sch
Redwood
Wilton Rd
Lower Lyndon Av
B5206
Coach House Dr
Old Lane
Hall Cl
Hope Crs
Fern Cl
Elnup Avenue
Elmfield
The Glade
Christleton
Broadlands
Foxfield Gv
Primary School
Central Dr
Gill Av
B5375 CHURCH LANE
BROAD O' TH' LANE
Braithwaite
Calico Wood Avenue
Miles Lane
Surgery
Manor Rd
Highfield Av
Houghton La
Clnc
PO
NEW MILES LANE
Shevington P School
M6
Gathurst Golf Club
Martland Av
Beechwood Avenue
Douglas Dr
Naylorfarm Av
Oakwood Av
Inward Drive
Dixon Dr
Dixon Av
Churchfield
Wood View
Ran Gall Avenue
St Anne's Dr
Vicarage Lane
Edgewood
The Oval
Works
WIGAN ROAD
B5375
GATHURST LANE
Woodlands Dr
Queensway
Prince's Park
Greenvale
Linley Cl
54
55
E
F
G
H
1
2
3
4
5
4
10
20
408
10
09

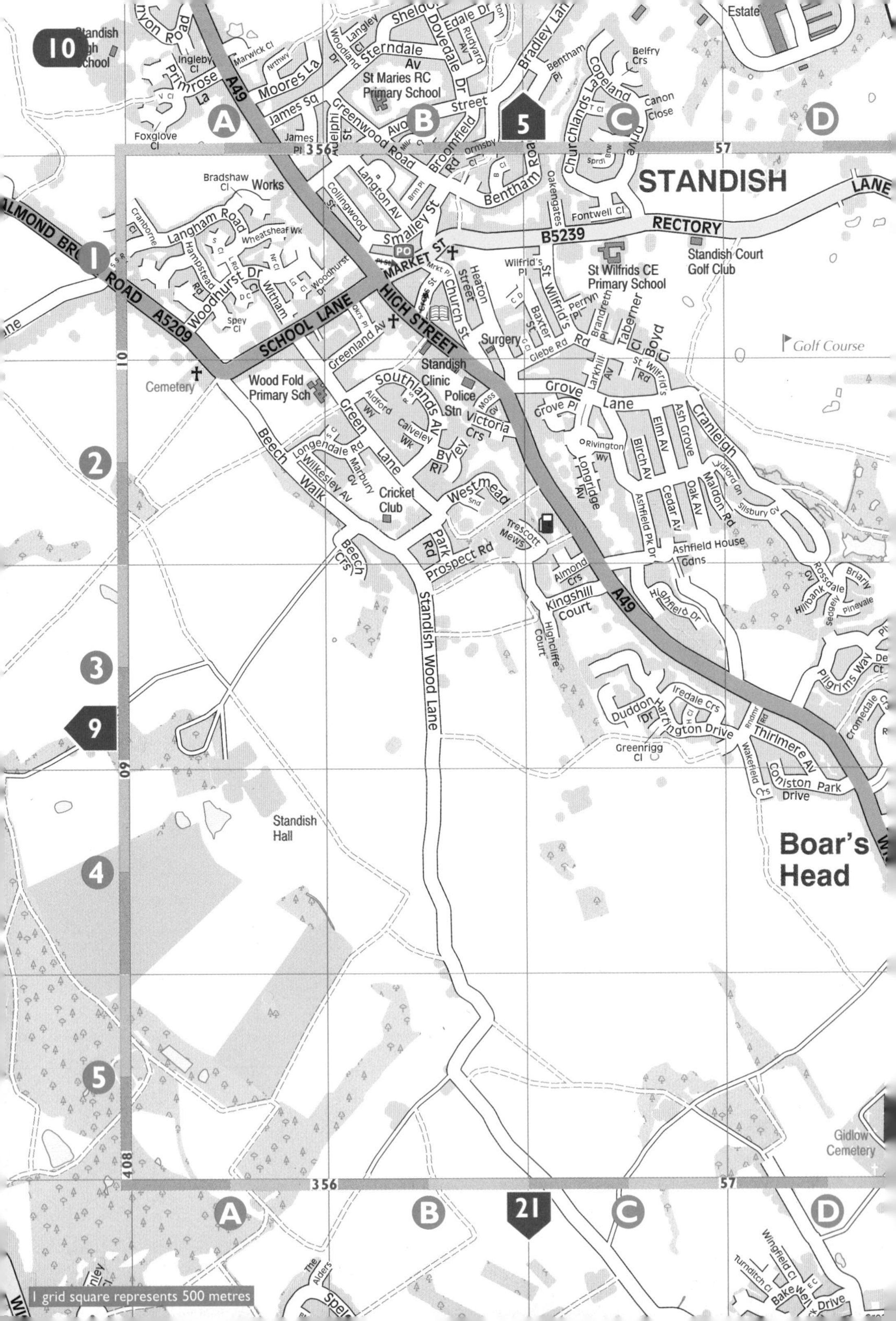

10
Standish High School
STANDISH
Boar's Head
A49
A5209
B5239
ALMOND BROOK ROAD
SCHOOL LANE
HIGH STREET
MARKET ST
RECTORY LANE
St Maries RC Primary School
St Wilfrids CE Primary School
Standish Court Golf Club
Golf Course
Wood Fold Primary Sch
Standish Clinic
Police Stn
Surgery
Cricket Club
Cemetery
Works
Standish Hall
Gidlow Cemetery
Estate
Standish Wood Lane
Beech Walk
Grove Lane
Green Lane
Southlands Av
Moores La
Sterndale Av
Greenwood Road
Broomfield Rd
Bentham Road
Bradley Lane
Churchlands La
Copeland Drive
Canon Close
Langham Road
Woodhurst Dr
Hampstead Rd
Witham
Smalley St
Langton Av
Collingwood St
Church St
Heaton Street
St Wilfrid's Rd
Baxter St
Glebe Rd
Taberner Cl
Boyd Cl
Cranleigh
Elm Av
Ash Grove
Birch Av
Cedar Av
Oak Av
Maldon Rd
Ashfield House Gdns
Longridge Av
Victoria Crs
Byley Ri
Westmead
Park Rd
Prospect Rd
Trescott Mews
Almond Crs
Kingshill Court
Highcliffe Court
Highfield Dr
Duddon Dr
Hartington Drive
Iredale Crs
Greenrigg Cl
Thirlmere Av
Coniston Park Drive
Wakefield Crs
Pilgrims Way
Cromedale Crs
Hillbank Gv
Rossdale
Briarly
Pinevale
Sedgely
Silsbury Gv
Lydford Gn
Fontwell Cl
Oakengates
Wilfrid's Pl
Perryn Pl
Brandreth Pl
Larkhill Av
Grove Pl
Rivington Wy
Longendale Rd
Wilkesley Av
Marbury Gv
Aldford Wy
Calveley Wk
Greenland Av
Beech Crs
Foxglove Cl
Primrose La
Ingleby Cl
Marwick Cl
James Sq
James Pl
Adelphi St
Edale Dr
Dovedale Dr
Rudyard Av
Woodland Dr
Langley
Bentham Pl
Belfry Crs
Bradshaw Cl
Cranborne Cl
Wheatsheaf Wk
Spey Cl
Moss Gv
Ormsby Cl
The Alders
Wingfield Cl
Turnditch Cl
Bakewell
356
57
408
09
10
A
B
C
D
1
2
3
4
5
9
21
1 grid square represents 500 metres

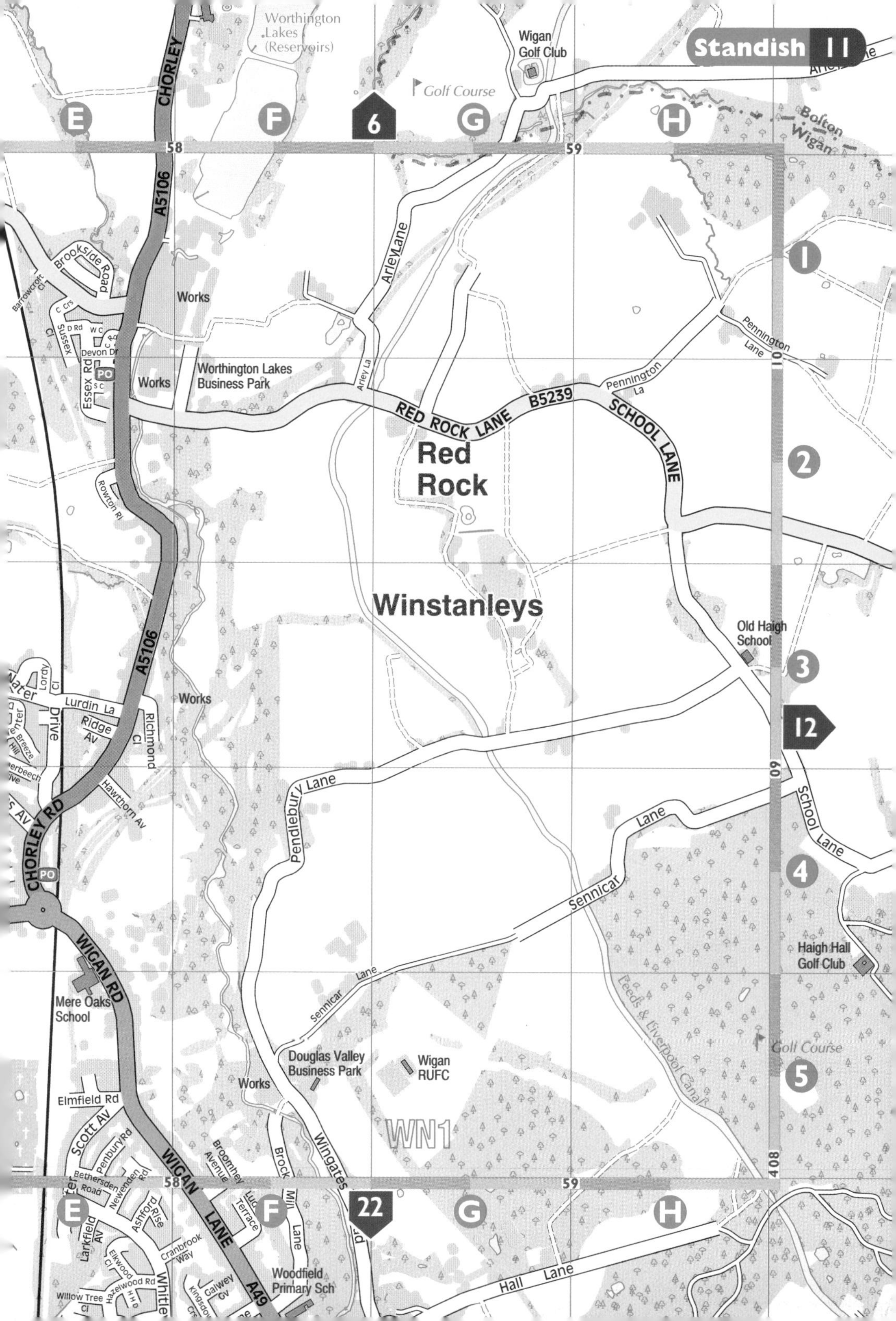
Worthington Lakes (Reservoirs)
Wigan Golf Club
Golf Course
6
E
F
G
H
Bolton Wigan
CHORLEY
A5106
58
59
Brookside Road
Barrowcroft Cl
Works
Sussex Cl
Devon Dr
Essex Rd
PO
Worthington Lakes Business Park
Arley Lane
Arley La
RED ROCK LANE
B5239
SCHOOL LANE
Pennington La
Pennington Lane
Red Rock
Rowton Rd
1
2
3
4
5
Winstanleys
Old Haigh School
12
Lurdin La
Lordy Cl
Ridge Av
Richmond Cl
Hawthorn Av
Drive
Pendlebury Lane
Lane
School Lane
Sennicar Lane
CHORLEY RD
WIGAN RD
Mere Oaks School
Haigh Hall Golf Club
Leeds & Liverpool Canal
Golf Course
Douglas Valley Business Park
Wigan RUFC
WN1
Elmfield Rd
Scott Av
Penbury Rd
Bethersden Road
Newenden Rd
Broomhey Avenue
Wingates
WIGAN LANE
A49
408
60
22
Ashford Rise
Larkfield Av
Elkwood Cl
Cranbrook Way
Hazelwood Rd
Willow Tree Cl
Galway Cv
Mill Lane
Woodfield Primary Sch
Hall Lane

12
Arley Lane
Lane
Scotland
Little Scotland
Blackrod Church School
Rd W
Bolton
Wigan
A
B
7
C
D
360
61
Little
Sibberings Farm
Bolton
Wigan
Copperas Lane
1
Tucker's Hill Brow
Tucker's Hill Farm
Pennington Lane
10
OL LANE
2
Toddington Lane
Meadow Pit Lane
Freezelan
Willoughbys
MEADOW PIT LANE
B5239
RILEY LANE
Old Haigh School
3
Haigh
HAIGH ROAD
B5239
Gorse Farm
11
St Davids CE Primary School
Stanley
Lane
09
Church St
School Lane
Copperas
Henley Street
Victoria Cl
B5239
Lane
Stancliffe Grove
Gorses Dr
4
HAIGH
Ratcliffe Road
St Mary's Road
ROAD
Parklands Dr
Calford
Haigh Hall Golf Club
Haigh Hall Country Park
New Road
St John's Rd
St Elizabeth's Road
Hilton Place
Copesthorne Cl
Ashfield Drive
St David's Crescent
Smith Street
Oakfield
Our Ladys RC Primary School
Greystone Crescent
Golf Course
Liverpool Canal
5
Council Building
Holly Rd
Lindsay Ter
Brayford
Aspull Clinic
Crawford Avenue
408
Manor Gv
Road
Balcarres
360
61
A
B
23
C
D
Crawford
Woods Road
Higher
1 grid square represents 500 metres

Works
Blackrod Station
Moss Lane
Cemetery
New Street
Vicarage Road
PO
Castlecroft Av
Vauze House
Chilgrove Av
Greenbarn
Thursford Grove
Shawbury Close
Manchester Road
Station Road
Hillside Avenue
Way
Corston Grove
Highfield Rd
Meadow Wy
B5408
Red Moss
Blackrod CP School
Greenbarn Way
Blackrod By-Pass Road
Park Hall Farm
Hope Street
The Cheethams
Scot Lane End CE School
Eskdale Av
Newlands Drive
Dorning Street
Scot Lane End
Scot Lane Industrial Estate
A6
Chorley Road
M61
Hilton House
Lane
Scot
Bolton
Wigan
Brinsop Hall Lane
Brinsop Hall
A6027
Cooper Turning
Dunoon Rd
Corfe Cl
Renfrew Rd
Lincoln Dr
Restormel Av
Old Fold Road
Drive
Criccieth Av
ASPULL
Conway Drive
Bolton
Dicconson Lane
Code
24
14
E
F
G
H
1
2
3
4
5
62
63
10
09
408

14
A
B
C
D
Fowler Industrial Estate
Thirlmere Avenue
Whitworth Street
Iron St
Telford Street
Bateman St
St Mary's RC Primary School
School
A673
PO
Balmoral Cl
Sandringham Road
Brunswick Avenue
Lancaster Av
Gloucester Av
Trevarrick Court
Makinson Av
Ainsworth Av
Beech Av
Brazley Avenue
Poplar Av
Laburnum Grove
Haskoll Street
Aspinall Street
Panton Street
CHORLEY NEW ROAD
Highland Rd
Derby St
Lindsay St
Old Greenwood La
Travers Street
Stanley Grove
Hollowell Lane
Sefton Lane
Cedar Avenue
St Josephs RC Secondary School
Ingersol Road
Springfield Road
Warner Village Cinema
Works
364
65
Red Moss
Futura Pk
Aspinall Way
Mansell Way
Enterprise Pk
Travers Street
Paragon Business Park
The Linkway
Hollywood Bowl
Greenpine Industrial Park
Reebok Museum
Green Pine Road
Burnden Way
Bolton Sports Arena
Bolton Running Track
Bolton Wanderers Football Club (Reebok Stadium)
A6027
Arena Approach
Hotel
Cranfield Road
Lostock Industrial Estate
Horwich Parkway
Hall
M61
13
Barton Fold Farm
Middle Brook
Lostock Lane
Lynstock
Junction 6
Lostock
ROAD
Brinsop Hall Lane
A6
Wingates Lane
Cooper Turning
408
409
410
1
2
3
4
5
B5239
Dicconson Lane
Fourgates County School
Dodd Lane Industrial Estate
Dodd Lane
25
Four Gates
CHORLEY
1 grid square represents 500 metres

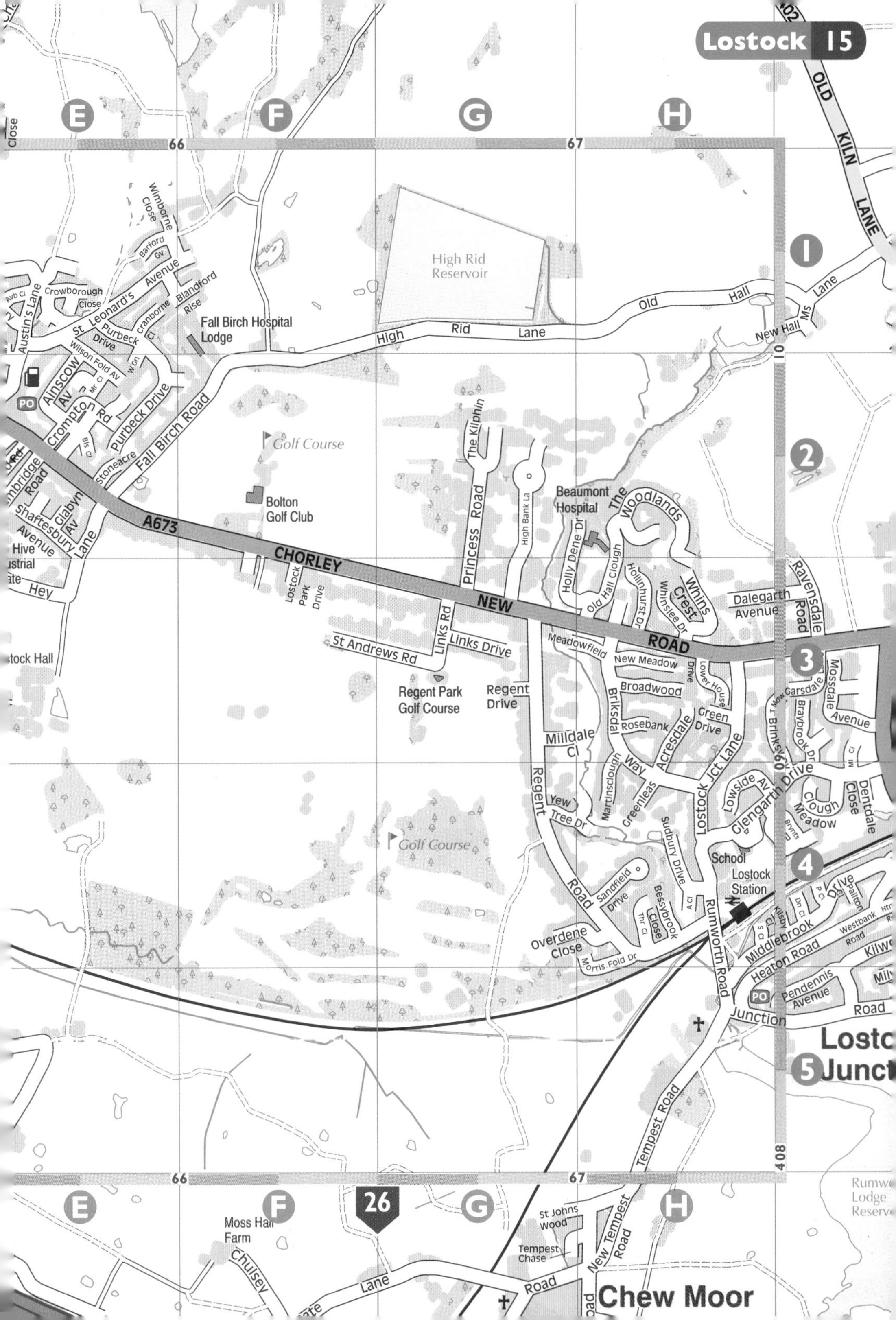
High Rid Reservoir
Fall Birch Hospital Lodge
High Rid Lane
Old Hall Lane
New Hall Ms
Old Kiln Lane
Golf Course
Bolton Golf Club
A673 Chorley New Road
Fall Birch Road
Princess Road
The Kilphin
High Bank La
Beaumont Hospital
The Woodlands
Holly Dene Dr
Old Hall Clough
Hollinhurst Dr
Whinslee Dr
Whins Crest
Dalegarth Avenue
Ravensdale Road
Lostock Park Drive
Links Rd
Links Drive
St Andrews Rd
Regent Park Golf Course
Regent Drive
Regent Road
Meadowfield
New Meadow
Broadwood
Briksdal Way
Rosebank
Acresdale
Green Drive
Lower House Drive
Milldale Cl
Martinsclough
Greenleas
Yew Tree Dr
Lostock Jct Lane
Sudbury Drive
Sandfield Drive
Bessybrook Close
Overdene Close
Morris Fold Dr
Rumworth Road
School
Lostock Station
Lowside Av
Glengarth Drive
Clough Meadow
Dentdale Close
Mosssdale Avenue
Garsdale
Braybrook Dr
Middlebrook Drive
Heaton Road
Westbank Road
Pendennis Avenue
Junction Road
Lostock Junction
Tempest Road
New Tempest Road
St Johns Wood
Tempest Chase
Chew Moor
Moss Hall Farm
Chulsey
Lane
Road
Rumworth Lodge Reservoir
St Leonard's Avenue
Crowborough Close
Austin's Lane
Purbeck Drive
Cranborne Cl
Blandford Rise
Wimborne Close
Barford Gv
Ainscow Av
Crompton Rd
Wilson Fold Av
Stoneacre
Glabyn Av
Shaftesbury Avenue
Lane
Hey
Lostock Hall
PO
66
67
E
F
G
H
26
408
410

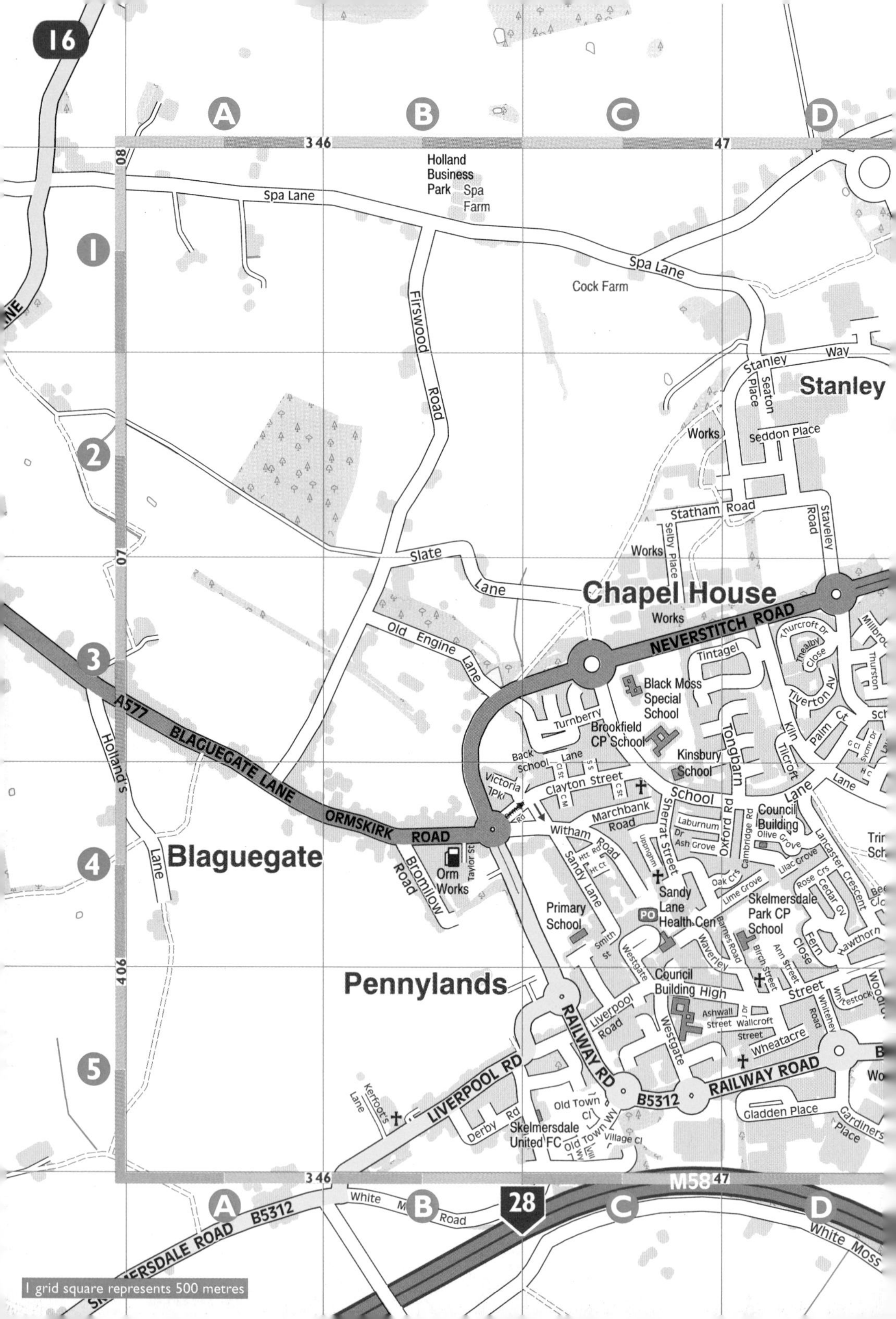

A
B
C
D
346
47
08
07
406
1
2
3
4
5
Holland Business Park
Spa Farm
Spa Lane
Cock Farm
Firswood Road
Stanley
Way
Stanley Place
Seaton
Seddon Place
Works
Statham Road
Staveley Road
Selby Place
Slate Lane
Chapel House
Old Engine Lane
NEVERSTITCH ROAD
Thurcroft Dr
Thealby Close
Tiverton Av
Tintagel
Black Moss Special School
Turnberry
Brookfield CP School
Kinsbury School
Tongbarn
Kiln
Tilcroft
Palm Ct
Lane
A577
BLAGUEGATE LANE
ORMSKIRK ROAD
Holland's Lane
Blaguegate
Back School Lane
Victoria
Clayton Street
Marchbank Road
Witham Road
Sandy Lane
School Lane
Sherrat Street
Oxford Rd
Cambridge Rd
Laburnum Dr
Ash Grove
Council Building
Olive Grove
Lancaster Crescent
Lilac Grove
Oak Crs
Lime Grove
Rose Crs
Cedar Gv
Bromilow Road
Taylor St
Orm Works
Primary School
Sandy Lane Health Cen
PO
Skelmersdale Park CP School
Fern Close
Hawthorn
Smith St
Westgate
Waverley
Barnes Road
Birch Street
Ann Street
Pennylands
Council Building
High Street
Whitestock
Whiteley Road
Ashwall Street
Wallcroft Street
Wheatacre
RAILWAY RD
Liverpool Road
LIVERPOOL RD
RAILWAY ROAD
B5312
Gladden Place
Gardiners Place
Kerfoot's Lane
Derby Rd
Old Town Cl
Old Town Wy
Village Cl
Skelmersdale United FC
M58
28
White Moss Road
B5312
SKELMERSDALE ROAD
White Moss
1 grid square represents 500 metres

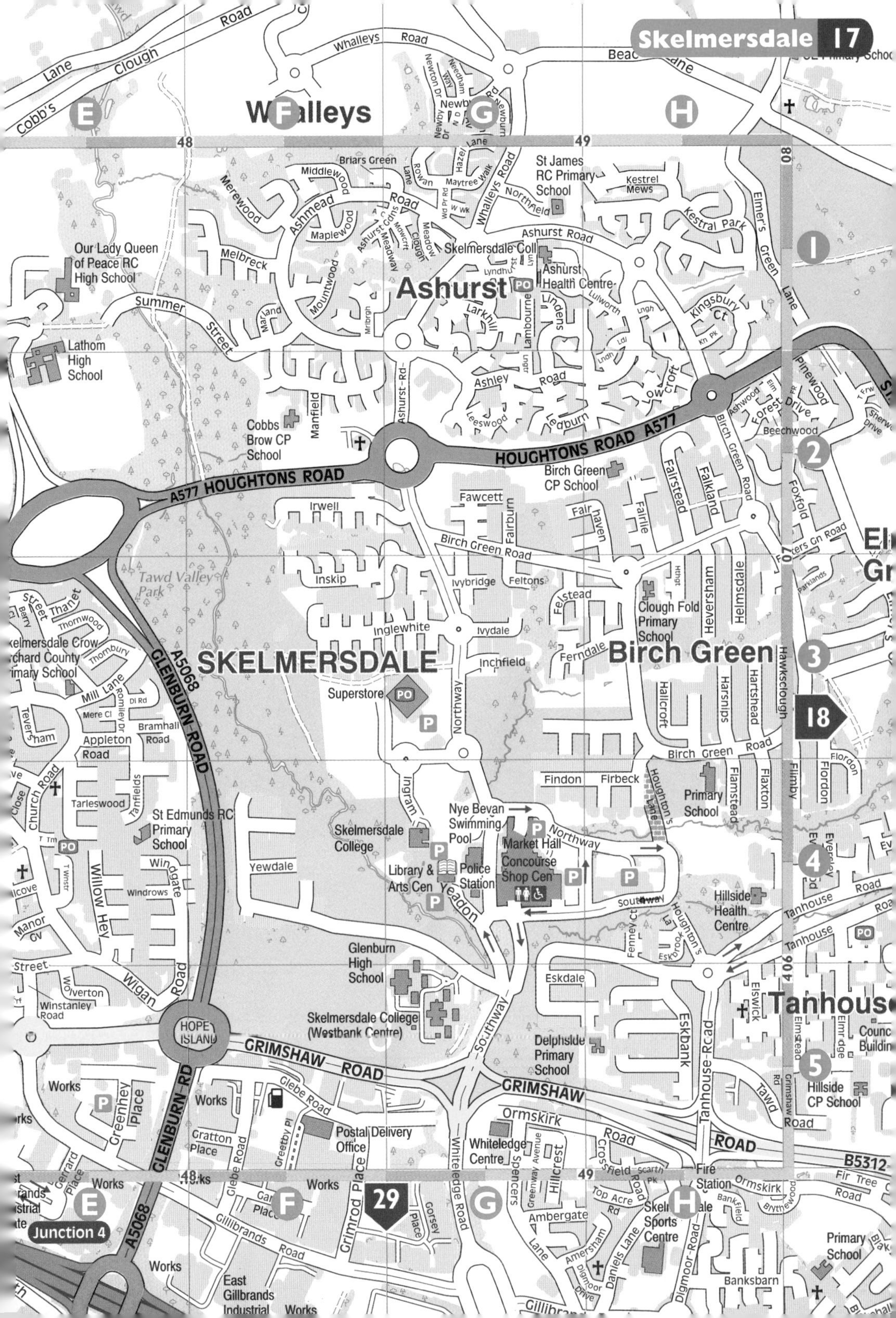
Whalleys
Whalleys Road
Clough Lane
Cobb's
Beacon Lane
Ashurst
SKELMERSDALE
Birch Green
Tanhouse
Tawd Valley Park
HOUGHTONS ROAD A577
A577 HOUGHTONS ROAD
GLENBURN ROAD A5068
GLENBURN RD
A5068
GRIMSHAW ROAD
GRIMSHAW
ROAD
B5312
Ormskirk Road
Birch Green Road
Ashurst Road
Summer Street
Northway
Southway
Yeadon
Tanhouse Road
Elmer's Green Lane
Gillibrands Road
Whiteledge Road
Wigan Road
Church Road
Mill Lane
Appleton Road
Glebe Road
Digmoor Road
Daniels Lane
Ashmead Road
Middlewood
Merewood
Melbreck
Maplewood
Mountwood
Marland
Manfield
Ashurst Rd
Lambourne
Lindens
Larkhill
Lulworth
Ashley Road
Leeswood
Ledburn
Lowcroft
Kingsbury Ct
Kestral Park
Kestrel Mews
Northfield
Whalleys Road
Briars Green
Rowan
Maytree Walk
Hazel Lane
Meadow Clough
Meadway
Ashurst Gdns
Pinewood
Forest Drive
Beechwood
Foxfold
Fosters Gn Road
Parklands
Fairstead
Falkland
Fairlie
Fairhaven
Fawcett
Fairburn
Irwell
Inskip
Ivybridge
Feltons
Felstead
Inglewhite
Ivydale
Inchfield
Ferndale
Heversham
Helmsdale
Hallcroft
Harsnips
Hartshead
Hawksclough
Flamstead
Flaxton
Flimby
Flordon
Findon
Firbeck
Houghton's Lane
Ingram
Yewdale
Eskdale
Eskbank
Eskbrook
Fenney Ct
Tanhouse Road
Elswick
Elmstead
Elmridge
Tawd
Grimshaw Rd
Eversley
Thanet Street
Berry Street
Thornwood
Thornbury
Tevers ham
Mere Cl
Romiley Dr
Dl Rd
Bramhall Road
Tarleswood
Tanfields
Windgate
Windrows
Willow Hey
Manor Gv
Wolverton
Winstanley Road
Greenhey Place
Gratton Place
Greetby Pl
Grimrod Place
Gorsey Place
Spencers Lane
Greenway Avenue
Hillcrest
Crossfield
Scarth Pk
Top Acre Rd
Ambergate
Amersham
Digmoor Drive
Bankfield
Blythewood
Fir Tree Road
Banksbarn
Our Lady Queen of Peace RC High School
Lathom High School
Cobbs Brow CP School
St James RC Primary School
Skelmersdale Coll
Ashurst Health Centre
Birch Green CP School
Clough Fold Primary School
Superstore
Primary School
Skelmersdale Crow Orchard County Primary School
St Edmunds RC Primary School
Skelmersdale College
Nye Bevan Swimming Pool
Market Hall
Concourse Shop Cen
Library & Arts Cen
Police Station
Hillside Health Centre
Glenburn High School
Skelmersdale College (Westbank Centre)
Delphside Primary School
Hillside CP School
Council Building
Postal Delivery Office
Whiteledge Centre
Fire Station
Skelmersdale Sports Centre
Works
East Gillbrands Industrial Works
Junction 4
HOPE ISLAND
E
F
G
H
I
2
3
4
5
48
49
08
07
406
18
29
PO
P

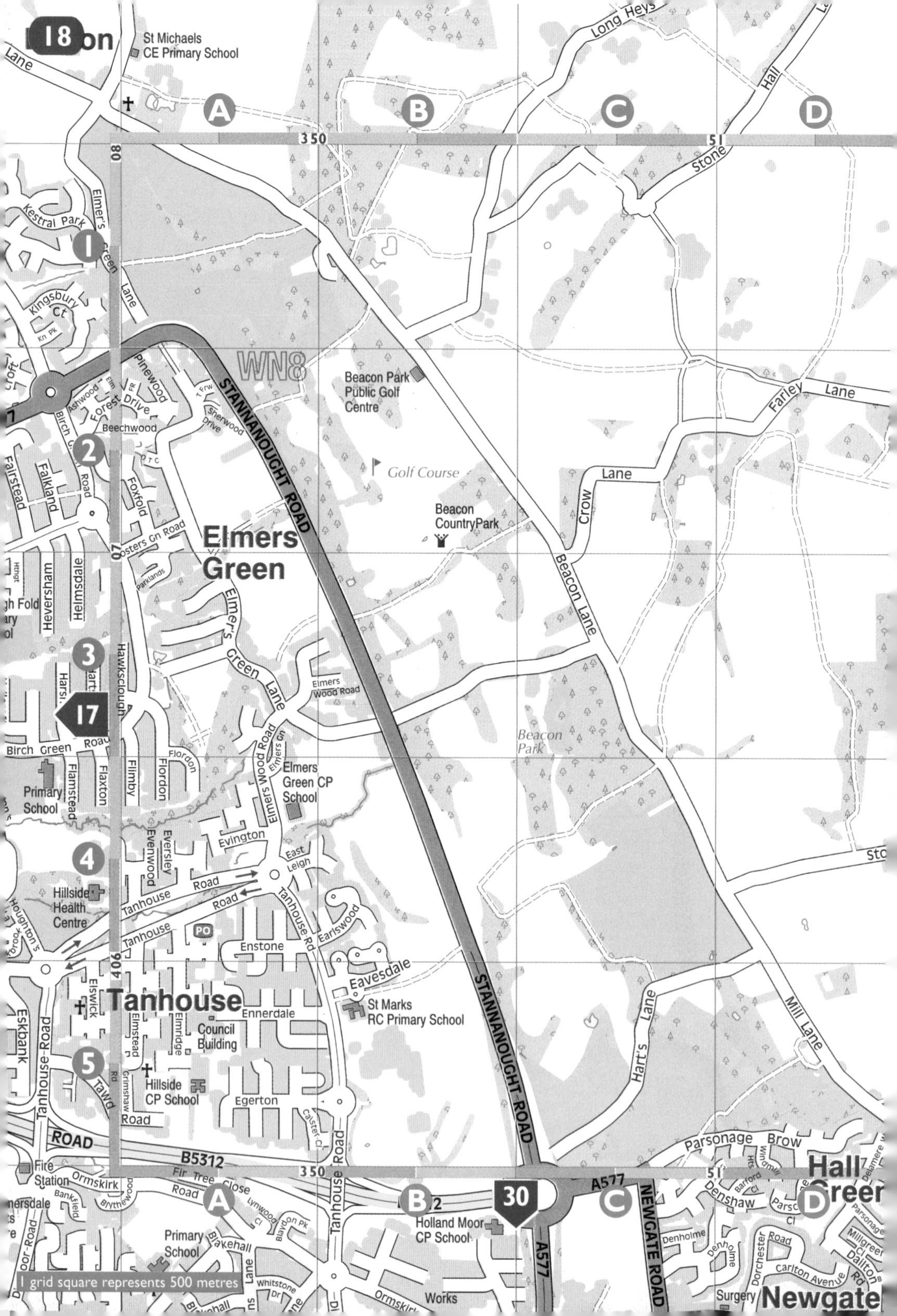
18
St Michaels
CE Primary School
Long Heys
Hall
Stone
Kestral Park
Elmer's Green Lane
Kingsbury Ct
WN8
STANNANOUGHT ROAD
Beacon Park
Public Golf
Centre
Farley Lane
Pinewood
Forest Drive
Beechwood
Sherwood Drive
Golf Course
Crow Lane
Fairstead
Falkland
Birch Green Road
Foxfold
Fosters Gn Road
Beacon
CountryPark
Elmers
Green
Beacon Lane
Heversham
Helmsdale
Parklands
Elmer's Green Lane
Hawksclough
Elmers Wood Road
17
Birch Green Road
Flordon
Beacon
Park
Elmers Wood Road
Elmers
Green CP
School
Primary
School
Flamstead
Flaxton
Filmby
Evington
Evenwood
Eversley
Hillside
Health
Centre
Tanhouse Road
East
Leigh
Tanhouse Rd
Earlswood
PO
Enstone
Eavesdale
St Marks
RC Primary School
Mill Lane
Hart's Lane
Tanhouse
Ennerdale
Council
Building
Eskbank
Tanhouse Road
Elmstead
Elmridge
Tawd Rd
Grimshaw Road
Hillside
CP School
Egerton
Caister Cl
Tanhouse Road
STANNANOUGHT ROAD
Parsonage Brow
ROAD
B5312
Fire
Station
Ormskirk Road
Fir Tree Close
Blythewood
Lynwood Cl
Blaydon Pk
350
30
A577
NEWGATE ROAD
Holland Moor
CP School
Hall
Green
Denshaw
Denholme
Dorchester Road
Carlton Avenue
Dalton Rd
Primary
School
Blakehall Lane
Whitstone Dr
Works
Ormskirk
Surgery
Newgate
1 grid square represents 500 metres

Holland Lees
Forest Fold Farm
Golf Course
Bank Top
Brow
Road
Ayrefield Lane
Roby Mill
Leeds & Liverpool Canal
M6
Gath
Cemetery
Roby Mill CE Sch
School Lane
Roby Mill
PO
Lafford Lane
Stoney Brow
Dean Wood
St Josephs RC College
Whitley Road
Brow
ROAD
Cathurst Road
GATHURST
College Road
St Theresa's School
Dean Wood Av
Golf Course
Spring Road
Lafford Lane
Dean Wood Golf Club
Hallbridge Gardens
A577
DINGLE ROAD
GROVE ROAD
Dingle Av
Hilldean
Woodside Cl
PARLIAMENT STREET
Derwent Road
Coniston Avenue
Windermere Rd
Oxford Rd
Harrow Cl
Thirlmere Av
Ullswater Av
Rydal Av
Thames Dr
Douglas Dr
Mersey Road
St Peters RC High
Orrell Post
Primary School
Surgery
Highgate Road
Grasmere Av
Rivington Drive
Dean Cl
Bridgehall Dr
Abbey Cl
Alma Hill
Hall Green
Priory Rd
Brookiands Road
Mill House Vw
Priory Nook
Spencer's Lane
Works
Oxton Av
Road
Way
Rugby Dr
Road
RK ROAD
8
20
31
2
3
4
5
E
F
G
H
I
52
53
08
07
406

Fold
20
Golf Course
Shevington
Vicarage Lane
9
A
B
C
D
Gathurst Lane
M6
Works
Crooke
Crooke Road
Gathurst
Gathurst Station
Ackhurst Lane
B5206
Ackhurst Hall
Martland Mill Industrial Estate
Cuthbert Scotts
Fourmarts Rd
Otterwood Square
19
St John Rigby College and Sports Centre
Walthew House La
Marsh Green
Spring Road
Gathurst Road
Dean Wood Av
Latham Lane
Wimborne Rd
Sherborne Rd
Mayfield Road
Dean Crescent
Prescott Lane
City Road
Bell Lane
Silverdale Road
Eccles Rd
Canberra Road
Beverley Road
Kitt
Comet
Cambridge Road
Derwent Road
Oxford Rd
Coniston Avenue
32
Norley Hall Cricket Club
Norley Road
Saddleback Road
Helvellyn Road
Heysham Road
Greenhey
Lamberhead Green County
Kingsdown High Sch
1 grid square represents 500 metres

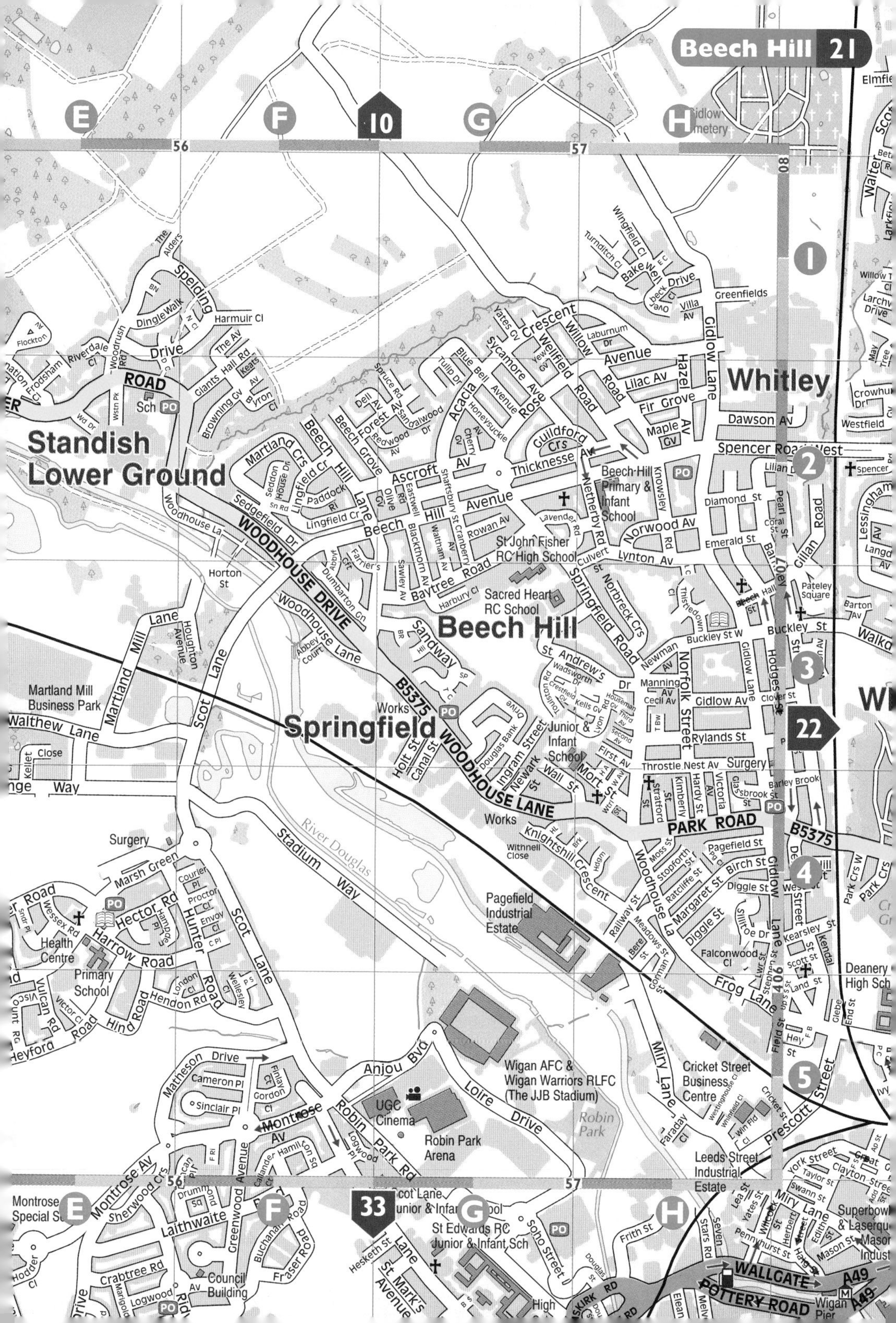
E
F
10
G
H
56
57
Gidlow Cemetery
I
Elmfield
Whitley
Standish Lower Ground
Beech Hill
Springfield
Spelding Drive
Dingle Walk
Harmuir Cl
Riverdale Cl
Woodrush Rd
Frodsham
Flockton Av
Giants Hall Rd
The Av
Keats Av
Byron Cl
Browning Gv
ROAD
Sch
PO
Woodhouse La
Sedgefield Dr
WOODHOUSE DRIVE
Woodhouse Lane
Horton St
Houghton Avenue
Martland Mill Lane
Scot Lane
Martland Mill Business Park
Walthew Lane
Kellet Close
Martland Crs
Seddon House Dr
Lingfield Cr
Paddock Ri
Beech Hill Lane
Beech Grove
Forest Av
Dell Av
Spruce Rd
Sandalwood Dr
Redwood Av
Tulip Dr
Blue Bell Avenue
Acacia Av
Cherry Gv
Honeysuckle Av
Sycamore Ave
Rose
Yates Gv
Crescent
Wellfield Road
Willow Road
Laburnum Dr
Avenue
Lilac Av
Hazel Av
Fir Grove
Maple Gv
Gidlow Lane
Greenfields
Villa Av
Overbeck Cl
Bakewell Cl
Drive
Wingfield Cl
Turnditch Cl
Dawson Av
Spencer Road West
Lilian Dr
Guildford Crs
Thicknesse Av
Netherby Rd
Beech Hill Primary & Infant School
Knowsley
Ascroft Av
Olive Gv
Eastwell Rd
Shaftsbury St
Hill Avenue
Beech
Rowan Av
Cranberry Av
Waltham Av
Blackthorn Av
Sawley Av
Baytree Road
Harbury Cl
Lavender Rd
St John Fisher RC High School
Sacred Heart RC School
Culvert St
Springfield Road
Norbreck Crs
Lynton Av
Norwood Av
Diamond St
Emerald St
Pearl St
Coral St
Gillan Road
Barrie St
Pateley Square
Buckley St
Buckley St W
Thistledown Cl
Newman Av
Manning Av
Cecil Av
Norfolk Street
Gidlow Lane
Hodges St
Gidlow Av
Rylands St
Clover St
22
Throstle Nest Av
Surgery
Barley Brook
Glassbrook St
Victoria Av
Hardy St
Kimberly
Stratford St
Dumbarton Gn
Farrier's Cft
Abbey Court
Sandway
Works
B5375
WOODHOUSE LANE
Canal St
Holt St
Douglas Bank Drive
Ingram Street
Newark St
St Andrew's Dr
Wadsworth Dr
Crestfield Dr
Kells Gv
Houseman Gv
Third Av
Second Av
First Av
Junior & Infant School
Wall St
Mort St
Lyon Rd
Works
PARK ROAD
Knightshill Crescent
Withnell Close
Woodhouse La
Moss St
Stopforth St
Ratcliffe St
Pagefield St
Birch St
Margaret St
Diggle St
Railway St
Meadows St
Bere St
Gorman St
Falconwood Cl
Frog Lane
Kearsley St
Kendal St
Scott St
Land St
Glebe
End St
Deanery High Sch
Hey St
Field St
Stephen St
Lwr St
5
Prescott Street
Cricket Street Business Centre
Cricket St
Westinghouse Cl
Whitfield Cl
Faraday Cl
Miry Lane
Leeds Street Industrial Estate
River Douglas
Stadium Way
Pagefield Industrial Estate
Wigan AFC & Wigan Warriors RLFC (The JJB Stadium)
Robin Park
Loire Drive
Anjou Bvd
UGC Cinema
Robin Park Arena
Robin Park Rd
Logwood Pl
Surgery
Marsh Green
Courier Pl
Proctor Cl
Envoy Cl
Hector Rd
Hampden Pl
Hunter Road
Scot Lane
Wessex Rd
Health Centre
Harrow Road
Primary School
Vulcan Rd
Viscount Rd
Heyford Rd
Victor Cl
Hind Road
Hendon Rd
London Cl
Wellesley
Matheson Drive
Finlay Cft
Cameron Pl
Gordon Cl
Sinclair Pl
Montrose Av
Callander
Hamilton Sq
Montrose Av
Sherwood Crs
Greenwood Avenue
Laithwaite
Buchanan Road
Fraser Road
Montrose Special Sch
33
Hesketh St
St Mark's Avenue
Ascot Lane Junior & Infant School
St Edwards RC Junior & Infant Sch
Soho Street
Douglas
Frith St
Crabtree Rd
Logwood Av
Council Building
Stars Rd
Lea St
Yates St
Pennyhurst St
Herbert St
Miry Lane
Swann St
Taylor St
York Street
Clayton Street
Superbowl & Laserquest
Mason St
WALLGATE
POTTERY ROAD
A49
Wigan Pier
Park Crs
Park Crs W
Walkden
Lessingham
Larchwood Drive
Crowhurst Dr
Westfield
Spencer
Walter Scott
Larkfield
Barton Av
Langdale Av
2
3
4

22
Gidlow Cemetery
Elmfield Rd
Douglas Valley Business Park
Works
Wigan RUFC
WN1
A
B
C
D
Penbury Rd
Broomhey Avenue
Wingates Road
Bethersden Road
Newenden Rd
Ashford Rise
Ludovic Terrace
Mill Lane
Walter
Larkfield Av
Cranbrook Way
Wigan Lane
A49
Woodfield Primary Sch
Hall Lane
Greenfields
Gidlow Lane
Villa Av
Hazel Grove
Willow Tree Cl
Hazelwood Rd
Larchwood Drive
Whitley Crescent
Galwey Gv
Kingsdown Crs
Sittingbourne Road
St Clement's Rd
Htl
Rose Bank Cl
Works
Leyland Mill La
Whitley
Marylebone
Crowhurst Dr
Westfield
Romney Wy
Brookland Road
Somerville Rd
Dawson Av
Spencer Road West
Spencer Road
Tennyson Dr
Milton Grove
Marylebone Pl
Lilian Dr
PO
Chaucer Pl
Mesnes Road
B5376
Diamond St
Pearl St
Coral St
Gillan Road
Lessingham
Cartmel Av
Danesway
Eskdale Av
Coniston Av
The Hollies
The Woodlands
Wordsworth Av
Emerald St
Holme Terrace
Green
Kingsmede
Bellingham Mt
Langdale Av
Hayes Av
Queensway
Heeley St
Stirling St
Alfred St
Inglewhite Av
A&E
Royal Albert Edward Infirmary
Bellingham Dr
Hotel
Bellingham Av
Halgh View
Woodland Grove
Rosemary Crs
Cedar Dr
Chestnut Road
Balniel Walk
Balcarres Av
Pateley Square
Barton Av
Rivington Av
Holme Av
Clifton Crs
New Ldg
Buckley St W
Buckley St
Walkden Avenue
Springfield St
Walnut Av
St Stephens Primary School
3
Norfolk Street
Hodges St
Street
Wilson Av
WIGAN
Kenyon Road
Copperfield
Swinley Lane
Swinley St
The Av
Kingsway
Widdrington Rd
Monument Rd
Whelley Hosp
Bradshaw Street
Gidlow Av
21
Hornby Street
Freckleton St
Fellside
West Mount
Moore St
Pyke St
Penketh St
Surgery
Swinley Road
Duke St
PO
Coppull Lane
Newton Cl
Wallace La
Lambert St
Greenacre
Rowanhill
Trafalgar Road
Avondale Rd
Shaw St
Earl St
Lord St
Charles St
Mesnes Park
Bridgeman Terrace
Dicconson St
Wrightington St
Scarisbrick St
Clifton St
Douglas Rd
Central Park Way
Kelway Ter
Alwyn St
Malpas Av
School Av
St East
Moore
Highfield Av
Park Road
B5375
Pagefield St
Delph St
Hill St
Parson's Walk
Eccleston St
Grayson's Cl
Mabs Cross Primary Sch
Riverside Av
Wynard Av
Alwyn Av
Gt Acre
Vine St
Ellis St
Sole St
4
Diggle St
Margaret St
West Street
Park Crs W
Park Crs
Cricket Ground
Surgery
Acton St
Superstore
Dicconson Ter
St Mary & St John RC Primary Sch
Perch Street
Northumberland Street
Bedford St
Falconwood Cl
Kearsley St
Kendal
Scott St
Council Building
School
Standishgate
Worsley Ter
Windsor St
Sullivan Way
Surg
Longshoot Close
Longshoot Hlt Cen
Essex St
Frog Lane
Deanery CE High Sch
Northway
B5376
Hilton St
Hotel
Regency Court
Greenough St
Scholes B5238
Stanley Place
Golborne Place
Kendrick Place
Wells Place
Postal Delivery Office
New Market St
Market St
The Galleries Shop Cen
Hallgate Bus Stn
River Way
Wigan Little Thtr
School Lane
Orchard St
Morris St
Isabella Square
Caunce Rd
Quarry Place
Scholes
Miry Lane
Cricket St Business Centre
Prescott Street
Business Cen
Marketgate Shopping Cen
Ship Yd
Millgate
Limefield
Butler St
Scholes Shop Pecinct
Scholefield Lane
Linney Square
5
Civic Cen
The Wiend Cen
PO
Jun Sch
Lorne St
Primary Sch
Leeds Street Industrial Estate
Wallgate Stn
King St West
Hardybutts
Birkett Bank
York Street
Clayton Street
Great George St
Taylor St
Wallgate
North W Stn
King St
Int Swim Pool
A49
Police
34
Silver Terrace
Cambridge Way
McCormack St
St Patricks Way
Hardybutts
East
59
Darlington Street East
Harper St
Miry Lane
Mason St
Super Bowl 2000
Queen Street
Pepper Mill Business Park
Magistrates Court
Sovereign Business Park
Leeds & Liverpool Canal
Mason Street Industrial Estate
Wallgate
Works
1 grid square represents 500 metres

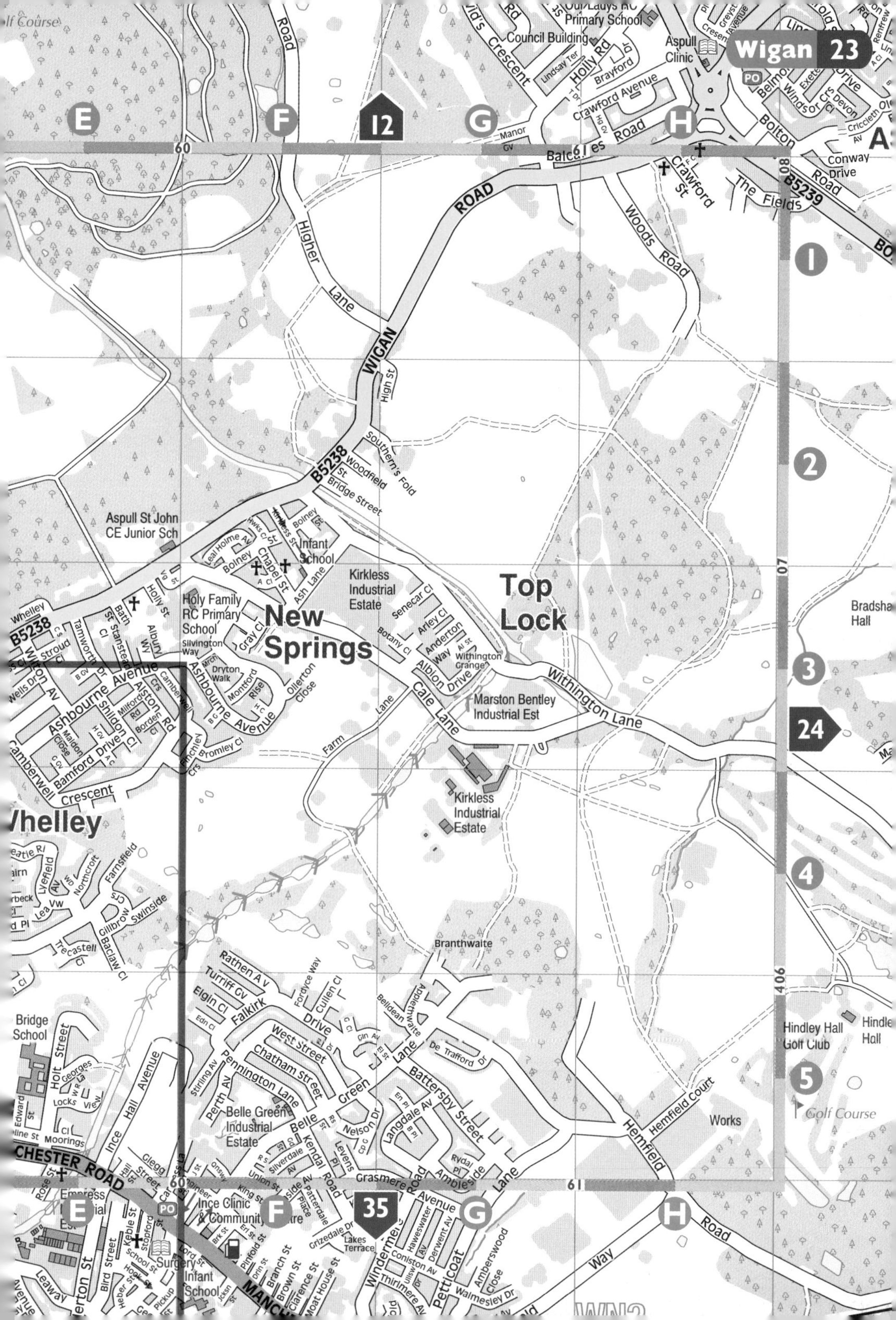
New Springs
Top Lock
Whelley
Wigan Road
B5238
B5239
Withington Lane
Higher Lane
Woods Road
Bolton Road
Balcarres Road
Aspull St John CE Junior Sch
Holy Family RC Primary School
Infant School
Kirkless Industrial Estate
Marston Bentley Industrial Est
Ashbourne Avenue
Hindley Hall Golf Club
Hindley Hall
Bradshaw Hall
Belle Green Industrial Estate
Bridge School
Ince Clinic & Community Centre
Manchester Road
Pennington Lane
Hemfield Road
Golf Course
Works
Branthwaite
12
24
35

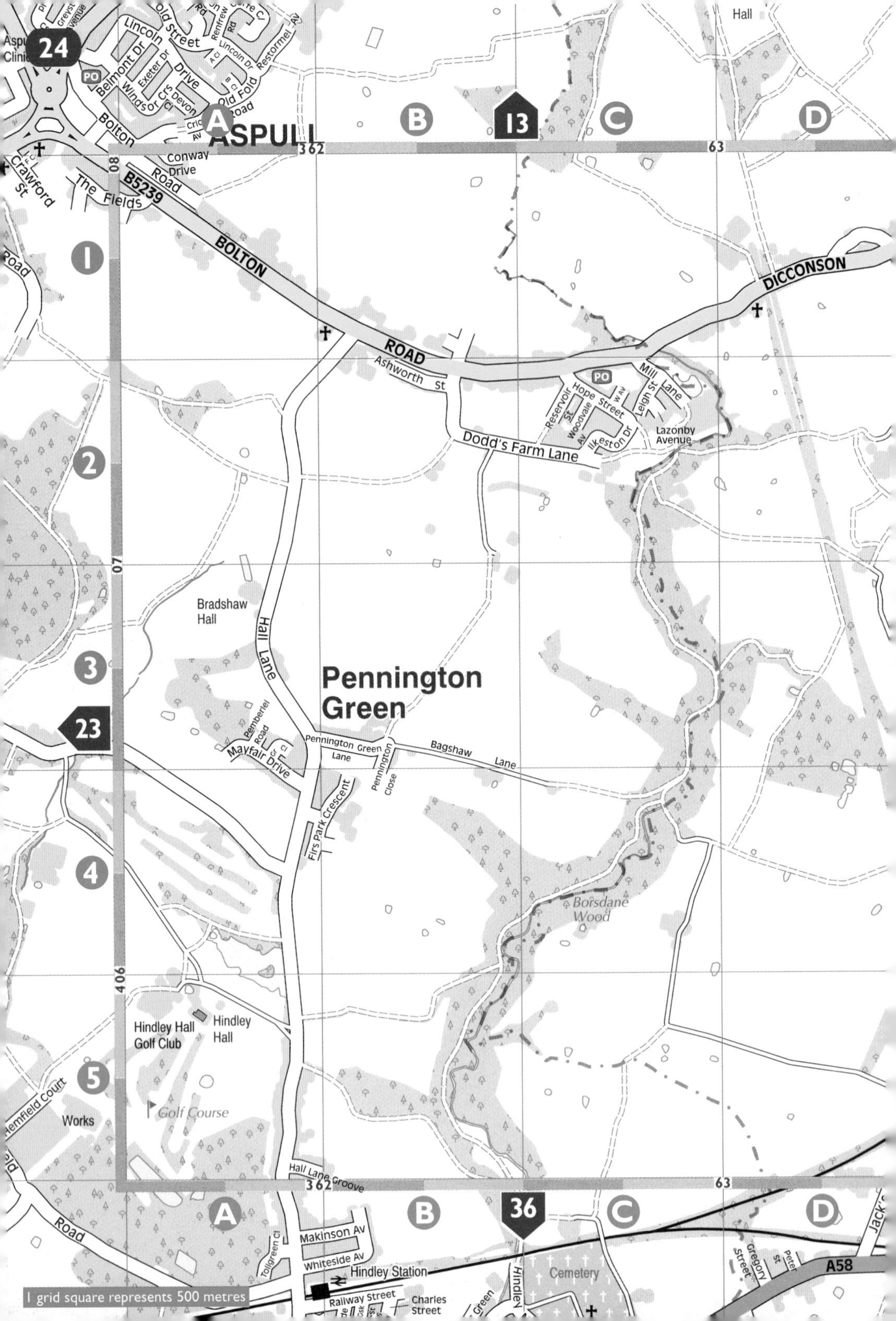
24
ASPULL
13
A
B
C
D
362
63
08
B5239
BOLTON ROAD
DICCONSON
Bolton Road
Conway Drive
The Fields
Crawford St
Lincoln Drive
Belmont Dr
Exeter Dr
Old Fold
Old Street
Restormel Av
Renfrew Rd
Devon Cl
Windsor Crs
Hall
Ashworth St
Dodd's Farm Lane
Reservoir St
Hope Street
Woodvale Av
Ilkeston Dr
Leigh St
Mill Lane
Lazonby Avenue
1
2
3
4
5
07
23
Bradshaw Hall
Hall Lane
Pennington Green
Pemberley Road
Mayfair Drive
Pennington Green Lane
Pennington Close
Bagshaw Lane
Firs Park Crescent
Borsdane Wood
406
Hindley Hall Golf Club
Hindley Hall
Golf Course
Works
Hemfield Court
Road
Hall Lane Groove
36
Makinson Av
Whiteside Av
Tollgreen Cl
Hindley Station
Railway Street
Charles Street
Hindley
Green
Cemetery
Gregory Street
Peter St
A58
1 grid square represents 500 metres

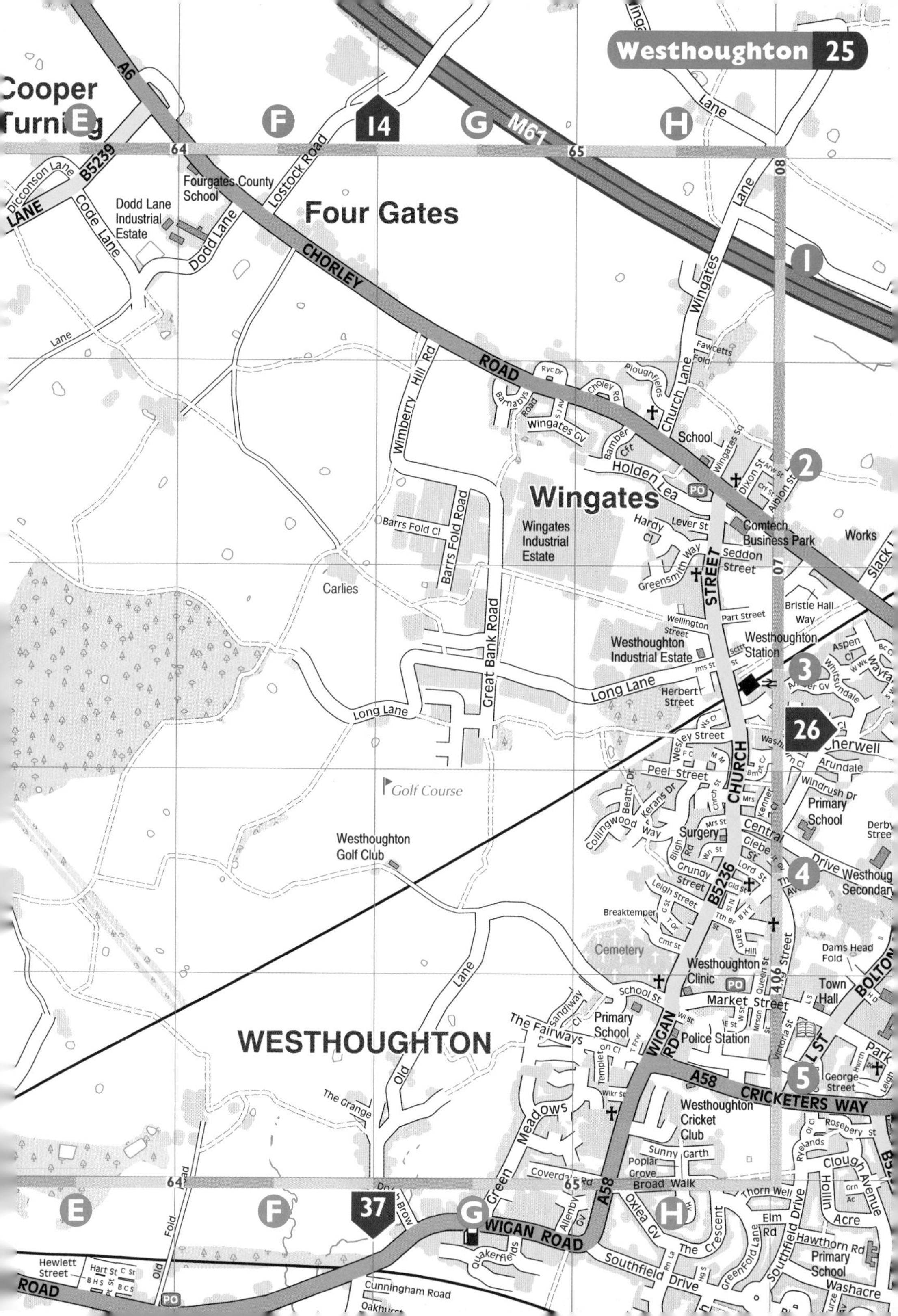
Cooper Turning
Four Gates
Wingates
WESTHOUGHTON
CHORLEY ROAD
WIGAN ROAD
CRICKETERS WAY
M61
A6
A58
B5239
B5236
Fourgates County School
Dodd Lane Industrial Estate
Dodd Lane
Lostock Road
Code Lane
Dicconson Lane
Wimberry Hill Rd
Barrs Fold Road
Barrs Fold Cl
Great Bank Road
Long Lane
Wingates Industrial Estate
Carlies
Golf Course
Westhoughton Golf Club
Wingates Lane
Church Lane
Fawcetts Fold
Ploughfields
School
Holden Lea
Hardy Cl
Lever St
Greensmith Way
Comtech Business Park
Works
Seddon Street
Part Street
Wellington Street
Westhoughton Industrial Estate
Westhoughton Station
Herbert Street
Bristle Hall Way
Aspen Cl
Whitsundale
Wesley Street
Peel Street
Beatty Dr
Kerans Dr
Collingwood Way
Surgery
Central Drive
Glebe St
Lord St
Grundy Street
Leigh Street
Breaktemper
Cemetery
Westhoughton Clinic
School St
Market Street
Police Station
Primary School
Arundale
Windrush Dr
Cherwell
Westhoughton Secondary
Dams Head Fold
Town Hall
George Street
Rosebery St
Ryelands
Clough Avenue
Hollin Acre
Hawthorn Rd
Primary School
Washacre
Southfield Drive
Greenfold Lane
The Crescent
Elm Rd
Thorn Well
Oxlea Gv
Sunny Garth
Poplar Grove
Broad Walk
Coverdale Rd
Westhoughton Cricket Club
Green Meadows
The Fairways
Sandiway Cl
Templeton Cl
The Grange
Old Lane
Old Fold Road
Allenby Gv
Quakerfields
Southfield Drive
Hewlett Street
Hart St
Cunningham Road
Oakhurst
BOLTON
Derby Street
Park
Slack
14
26
37
E F G H I
2 3 4 5
64 65 07 08

26
15
25
38
A
B
C
D
366
67
08
07
406
Moss Hall Farm
Chulsey Gate Lane
Wingates Lane
Tempest Road
New Tempest Road
St Johns Wood
Tempest Chase
Chew Moor
Havisham Cl
Copperfields
Lock Lane
Oakbarton
St John's Road
Pocket Nook Rd
Meadowbrook Close
Fawcetts Fold
Church Lane
School
Wingates Sq
PO
Lever St
Dixon St
Albion St
Comtech Business Park
Works
Slack Lane
Seddon Street
Part Street
Wellington Street
Westhoughton Station
Herbert Street
Bristle Hall Way
Ingleby Cl
Glazebury Dr
Metal Box Way
Chew Moor Lane
M61
Winslow
MANCHESTER ROAD
Aspen Cl
Wayfaring
Whitsundale
Amber Gv
Churnett Cl
Wharfedale
Broom Way
Heatons Grove
Farilegh Cl
Snydale Close
Bolton Road
Calver Hey Close
White Horse Gv
Wesley St
Peel Street
Cherwell Road
Arundale
Windrush Dr
Primary School
Washburn Cl
Bolton Road Industrial Estate
Chelmer Close
B5235
Allesley Cl
Derby Street
Surgery
Central Drive
Glebe St
Hall Lee Dr
Cow Lees
Upper Lees Dr
Allerton Cl
Lodge Dr
Yellow
Molyneux Road
A6
Manley Crs
Manchester Rd
A58 Snydale
Che
Chequerbe Works
Grundy Street
Leigh Street
Westhoughton County Secondary School
The Avenue
Winterton Close
Selbourne Cl
Lees Road
Fellbridge Cl
Barnfield Dr
St Thomas CE Primary School
Beehive Gn
Singleton Gv
Captain Lees
Fairhaven Av
Alexandria Dr
Brancker Street
Westhoughton Clinic
Dams Head Fold
BOLTON ROAD
Westhoughton High School and Community Leisure Centre
King Street
Town Hall
Market Street
Park Meadow
Dale Lee
Captain Lees Gdns
A58 Park Road
Water's Nook
WIGAN RD
Police Station
Victoria St
MILL ST
Park Road
Alma Road
George Street
Surgery
Balley Fold
Lee Bank
A58 CRICKETERS WAY
Westhoughton Cricket Club
Forest Drive
Medical Centre
Rosebery St
Ryelands
Wade Bank
Dalton Fold
B5235
Bank Side
BL5
Sunny Garth
Clough Ave
Thorn Well
Elm Rd
The Crescent
Southfield Drive
Hawthorn Rd Primary School
LEIGH ROAD
Landedmans
Stanley Cl
Roscoe Court
Washacre Close
Hooper Green
Bank Field
1 grid square represents 500 metres

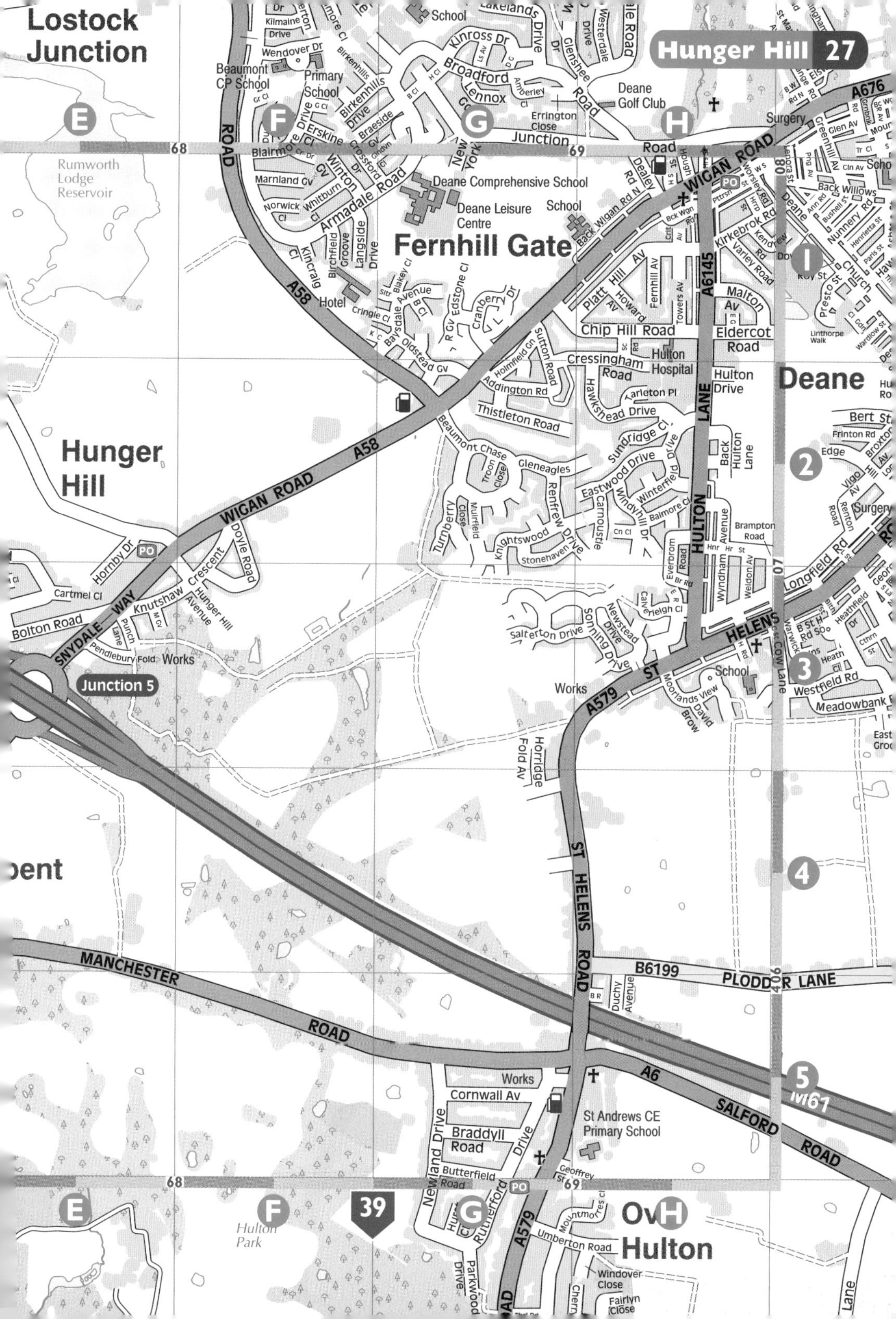

Lostock Junction
Rumworth Lodge Reservoir
Beaumont CP School
Primary School
School
Kinross Dr
Broadford
Lennox
Lakelands Drive
Glenshee Drive
Westerdale Drive
Deane Golf Club
Errington Close
Junction Road
New York
Deane Comprehensive School
Deane Leisure Centre
Fernhill Gate
WIGAN ROAD
A58
A676
A6145
Surgery
Blairmore Cl
Erskine Cl
Winton Gv
Crossford Dr
Armadale Road
Marnland Gv
Norwick Cl
Whitburn Cl
Kincraig Cl
Birchfield Groove
Langside Drive
Hotel
Cringle Cl
Baysdale Avenue
Oldstead Gv
Edstone Cl
Cranberry Dr
Back Wigan Rd N
Dealey Rd
Platt Hill Av
Howard Av
Fernhill Av
Towers Av
Kirkebrok Rd
Varley Road
Malton Av
Eldercot Road
Chip Hill Road
Hulton Hospital
Cressingham Road
Sutton Road
Holmfield Gn
Addington Rd
Thistleton Road
Hawkshead Drive
Carleton Pl
Hulton Drive
HULTON LANE
Back Hulton Lane
Deane
Bert St
Frinton Rd
Edge
Vigo Av
Renton Road
Surgery
Longfield Rd
Hunger Hill
Beaumont Chase
Troon Close
Gleneagles
Renfrew Drive
Sundridge Cl
Eastwood Drive
Winterfield Drive
Windyhill Dr
Balmore Cl
Carnoustie
Turnberry
Muirfield Close
Knightswood
Stonehaven
Brampton Road
Wyndham Avenue
Weldon Av
Everbrom Road
Calverleigh Cl
Salterton Drive
Sonning Drive
Newstead Drive
Hornby Dr
PO
Doyle Road
Crescent
Knutshaw
Hunger Hill Avenue
Cartmel Cl
Bolton Road
SNYDALE WAY
Punch Lane
Pendlebury Fold
Works
Junction 5
ST HELENS
A579
School
Moorlands View
David Brow
Cow Lane
Westfield Rd
Meadowbank
Heathfield
Horridge Fold Av
ST HELENS ROAD
B6199
PLODDER LANE
Duchy Avenue
MANCHESTER ROAD
A6
SALFORD ROAD
M61
Works
Cornwall Av
Braddyll Road
Newland Drive
Butterfield Road
Rutherford Drive
St Andrews CE Primary School
Geoffrey St
Hulton Park
Over Hulton
Umberton Road
Windover Close
Fairlyn Close
Parkwood Drive
Lane
68
69
07
06
39
E
F
G
H
I
2
3
4
5

LIVERPOOL RD
Kerfoot's Lane
Derby Rd
RAILWAY RD
Old Town Cl
Old Town Wy
Westgate
Street
Wheatacre
B5312
RAILWAY ROAD
Gladden Place
Gardiners Place
Work
A
B
16
C
D
346
47
M58
White Moss Road
SKELMERSDALE ROAD B5312
1
Stanley Farm
05
M58
2
Rainford Road
A570(T)
3
04
RAINFORD ROAD
Coal Pit Lane
Holly Lane
4
5
Holly Fold Farm
News Lane
403
346
47
A
B
42
C
D
Ben Lane Farm
Ben Lane Court
Park
1 grid square represents 500 metres

Digmoor 29
HOPE ISLAND
GRIMSHAW ROAD
(Westbank Centre)
Delphside Primary School
Hillside CP School
Works
Greenhey Place
GLENBURN RD
Glebe Road
Gratton Place
Postal Office
17
Ormskirk Road
Crossfield Road
Fire Station
B5312
Fir Tree Road
Works
Garnett Place
Grimrod Place
Gorsey Place
Whiteledge Road
Spencers Lane
Hillcrest
Ambergate
Top Acre Rd
Skelmersdale Sports Centre
Daniels Lane
Digmoor Road
Primary School
Junction 4
A5068
Gillibrands Road
East Gillbrands Industrial Estate
Amersham
Digmoor Drive
Banksbarn
Blakehall
Beechtrees
Abbeywood
Acregate
Infant School
Digmoor
Surgery
Moss Lane View
M58
Little Digmoor CP School
Bearncroft
Alderley
Birkrig
Moss Lane
White Moss Farm
Whiteledge Road
Road
Pennine Pl
Pimbo
Holland Moss
Nipe Lane
Works
Pikelaw Place
Pilling Place
Penketh Place
Pimbo Road
Pit Hey Place
Paddock Road
30
Ferny Knoll
Ferny Knoll Road
Lancashire County
St. Helens
Holland Moss
Paxton Place
Place
Duke's
Wood
48
49
05
04
403
Rainford Junction
43
Crawford
News Lane

30
Council Building
Hillside CP School
Egerton
Tawd Road
ROAD
A
B
18
C
D
Parsonage Brow
B5312
350
51
Hall Green
Fire Station
Ormskirk Road
Fir Tree Close
Holland Moor CP School
A577
NEWGATE ROAD
Denshaw
Primary School
Blakehall
Tanhouse Road
Digmoor Road
Works
Ormskirk Road
Newgate
Surgery
Moorside CP Sch
Back Lane
Ormskirk Road
Digmoor
Infant School
Birleywood Health Cen
Surgery
Clay Brow Road
Brick Works
1
2
3
4
5
M58
St Lukes RC Primary Sch
Pimbo Road
Chequer Lane
Tower Hill Road
Junction 5
Works
Industrial Estate
STANNANOUGHT ROAD
Hotel
29
Prescott Road
Up Holland Station
Pimbo Lane
Long Lane
Crawford County Sch
Duke's Wood
Millets
44
Crawford
1 grid square represents 500 metres

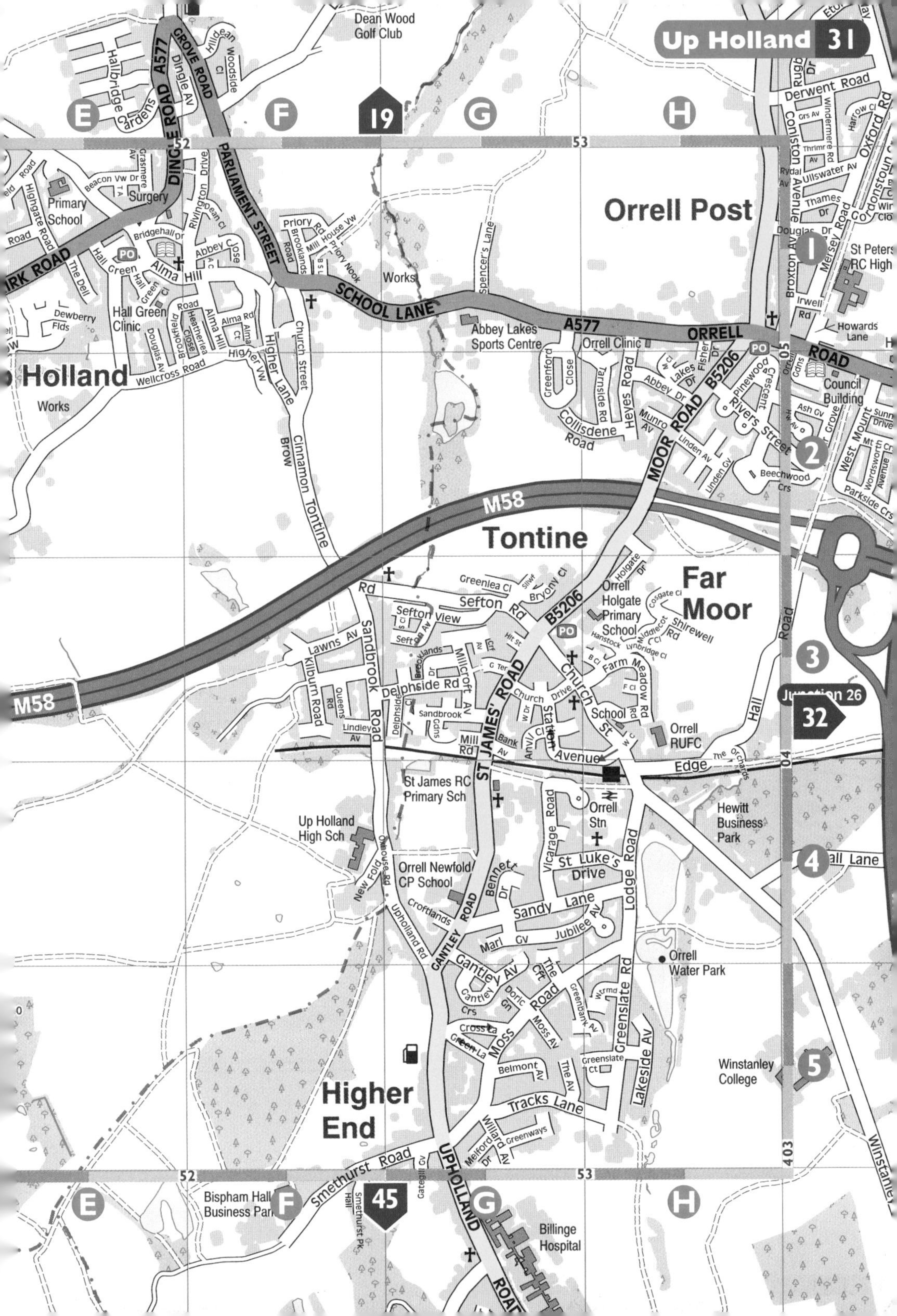
Dean Wood Golf Club
19
E
F
G
H
52
53
Orrell Post
Up Holland
Tontine
Far Moor
Higher End
M58
A577
B5206
SCHOOL LANE
ORRELL ROAD
PARLIAMENT STREET
GROVE ROAD
DINGLE ROAD
MOOR ROAD
ST JAMES' ROAD
GANTLEY ROAD
UPHOLLAND ROAD
Primary School
Surgery
Hall Green Clinic
Works
Abbey Lakes Sports Centre
Orrell Clinic
St Peters RC High
Council Building
Orrell Holgate Primary School
Orrell RUFC
St James RC Primary Sch
Up Holland High Sch
Orrell Newfold CP School
Orrell Stn
Hewitt Business Park
Orrell Water Park
Winstanley College
Bispham Hall Business Park
Billinge Hospital
Junction 26
32
45
Cinnamon Tontine
Higher Lane
Church Street
Spencer's Lane
Sandbrook Road
Kilburn Road
Sefton Rd
Delphside Rd
Millcroft Av
Church Drive
Station Avenue
Farm Meadow Rd
Shirewell Rd
Hall Road
Edge Hall Lane
Lodge Road
Vicarage Road
St Luke's Drive
Sandy Lane
Jubilee Av
Marl Gv
Gantley Av
Moss Road
Greenslate Rd
Lakeside Av
Tracks Lane
Smethurst Road
Collisdene Road
Heyes Road
Rivers Street
Derwent Road
Coniston Avenue
Mersey Road
Oxford Rd
Wellcross Road
Alma Hill
403
04
05
1
2
3
4
5

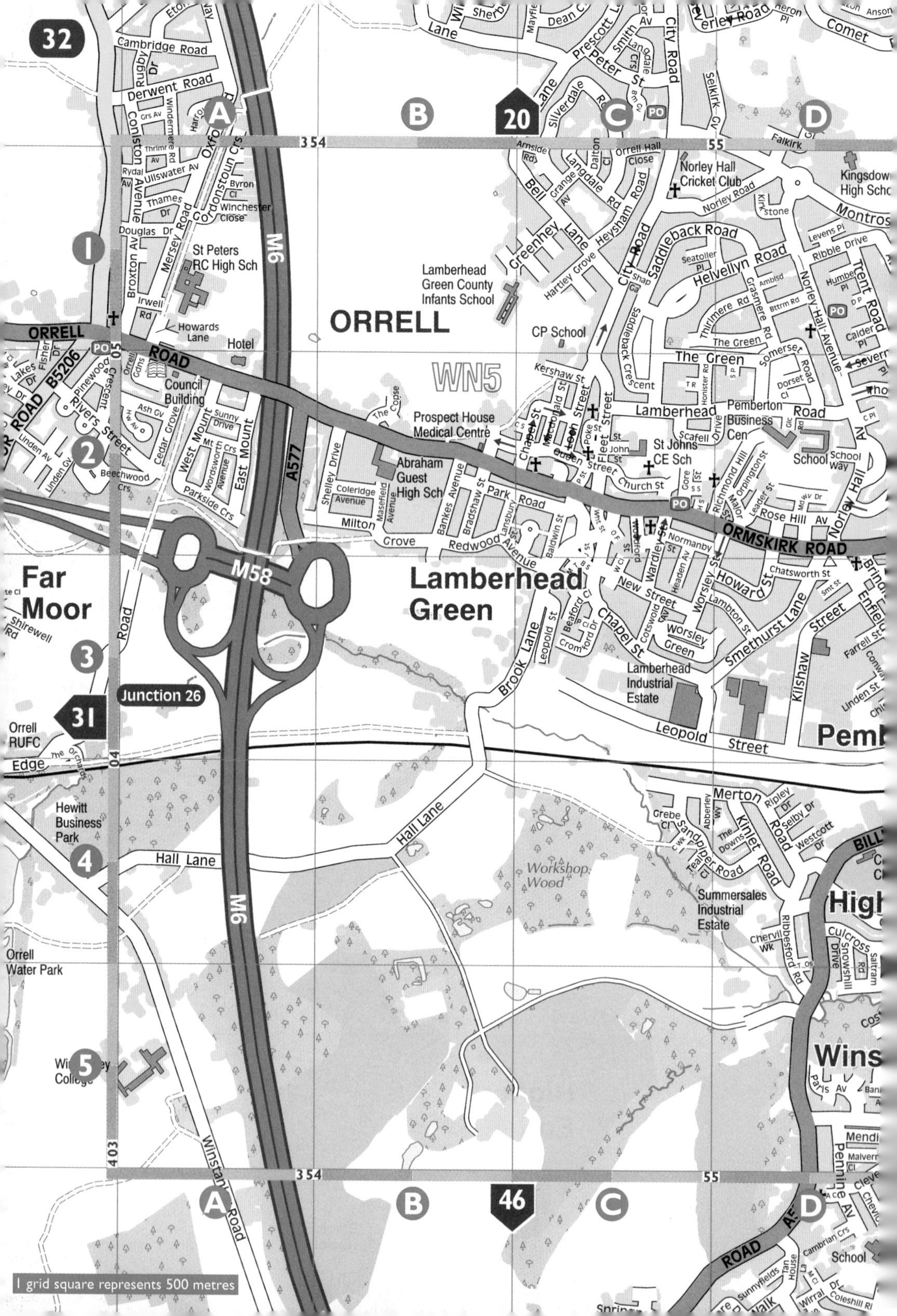
ORRELL
WN5
Lamberhead Green
Far Moor
Orrell RUFC
Hewitt Business Park
Orrell Water Park
Junction 26
M6
M58
A577
B5206
ORRELL ROAD
ORMSKIRK ROAD
St Peters RC High Sch
Howards Lane
Hotel
Council Building
Lamberhead Green County Infants School
CP School
Prospect House Medical Centre
Abraham Guest High Sch
St Johns CE Sch
Pemberton Business Cen
School
Norley Hall Cricket Club
Kingsdown High Scho
Lamberhead Industrial Estate
Summersales Industrial Estate
Workshop Wood
Leopold Street
Hall Lane
Winstanley Road
Brook Lane
Chapel St
City Road
Saddleback Road
Helvellyn Road
Norley Hall Avenue
Norley Road
Lamberhead Road
The Green
Smethurst Lane
Kilshaw Street
Merton Road
Kinlet Road
Sandpiper Road
Cambridge Road
Derwent Road
Coniston Avenue
Mersey Road
Gordonstoun Crs
Cedar Grove
West Mount
East Mount
Park Road
Redwood Avenue
Milton Grove
Shelley Drive
Bankes Avenue
Bradshaw St
New Street
Wardley St
Worsley St
Howard St
Rose Hill Av
Worsley Green
Edge
Pemb
High
Wins
1 grid square represents 500 metres

20
31
46

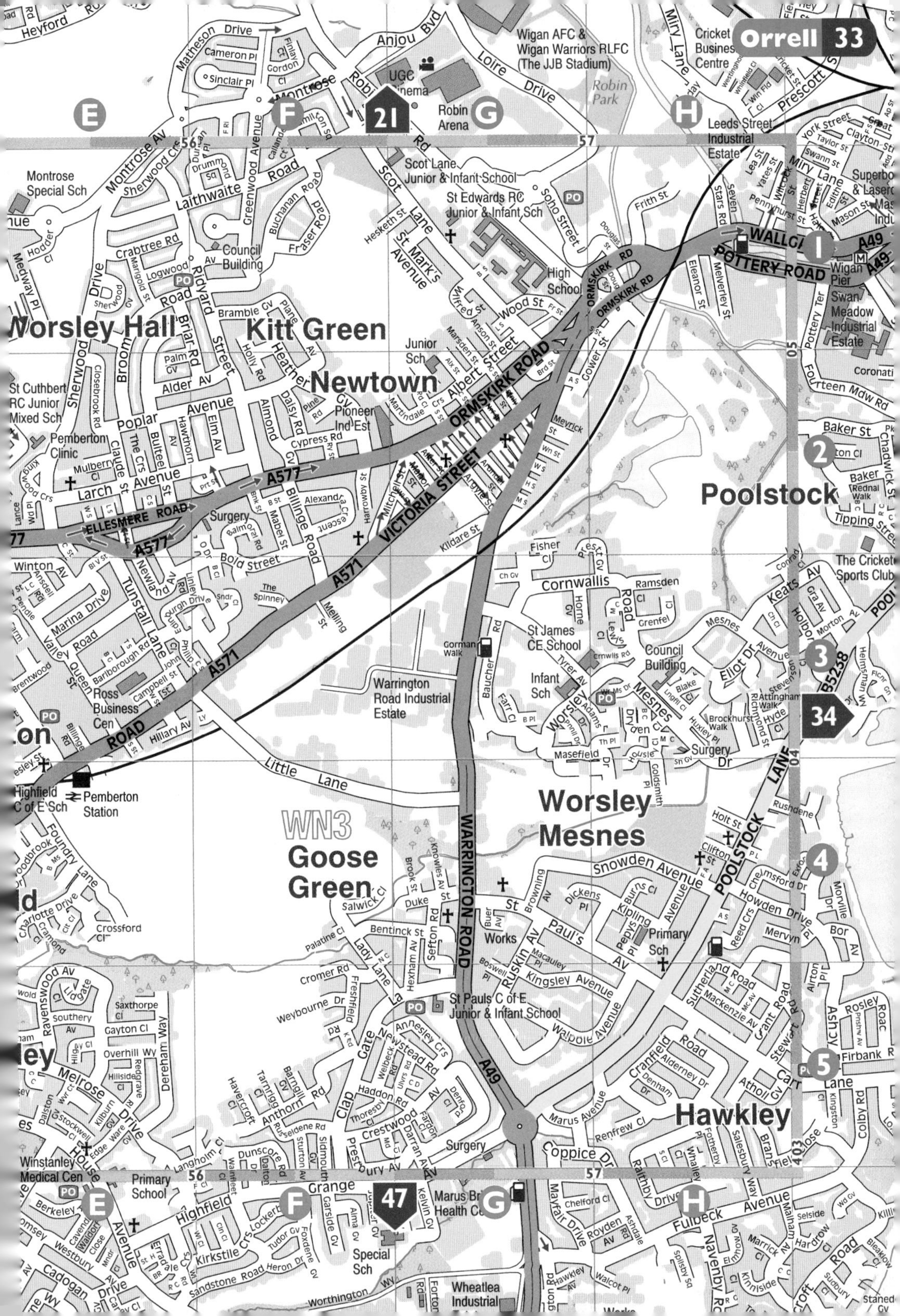
Worsley Hall
Kitt Green
Newtown
Poolstock
Worsley Mesnes
Goose Green
Hawkley
WN3
Wigan AFC &
Wigan Warriors RLFC
(The JJB Stadium)
Robin Park
Robin Arena
UGC Cinema
Cricket Business Centre
Leeds Street Industrial Estate
Wigan Pier
Swan Meadow Industrial Estate
Scot Lane Junior & Infant School
St Edwards RC Junior & Infant Sch
High School
Junior Sch
Pioneer Ind Est
Montrose Special Sch
Council Building
St Cuthbert RC Junior Mixed Sch
Pemberton Clinic
Surgery
Ross Business Cen
Highfield C of E Sch
Pemberton Station
Warrington Road Industrial Estate
St James CE School
Infant Sch
The Cricketer Sports Club
Primary Sch
St Pauls C of E Junior & Infant School
Works
Winstanley Medical Cen
Primary School
Marus Bridge Health Cen
Special Sch
Wheatlea Industrial
ORMSKIRK ROAD
VICTORIA STREET
ELLESMERE ROAD
WARRINGTON ROAD
POTTERY ROAD
POOLSTOCK LANE
Little Lane
A577
A571
A49
B5238
21
34
47
E
F
G
H
56
57
05
04
403
2
3
4
5

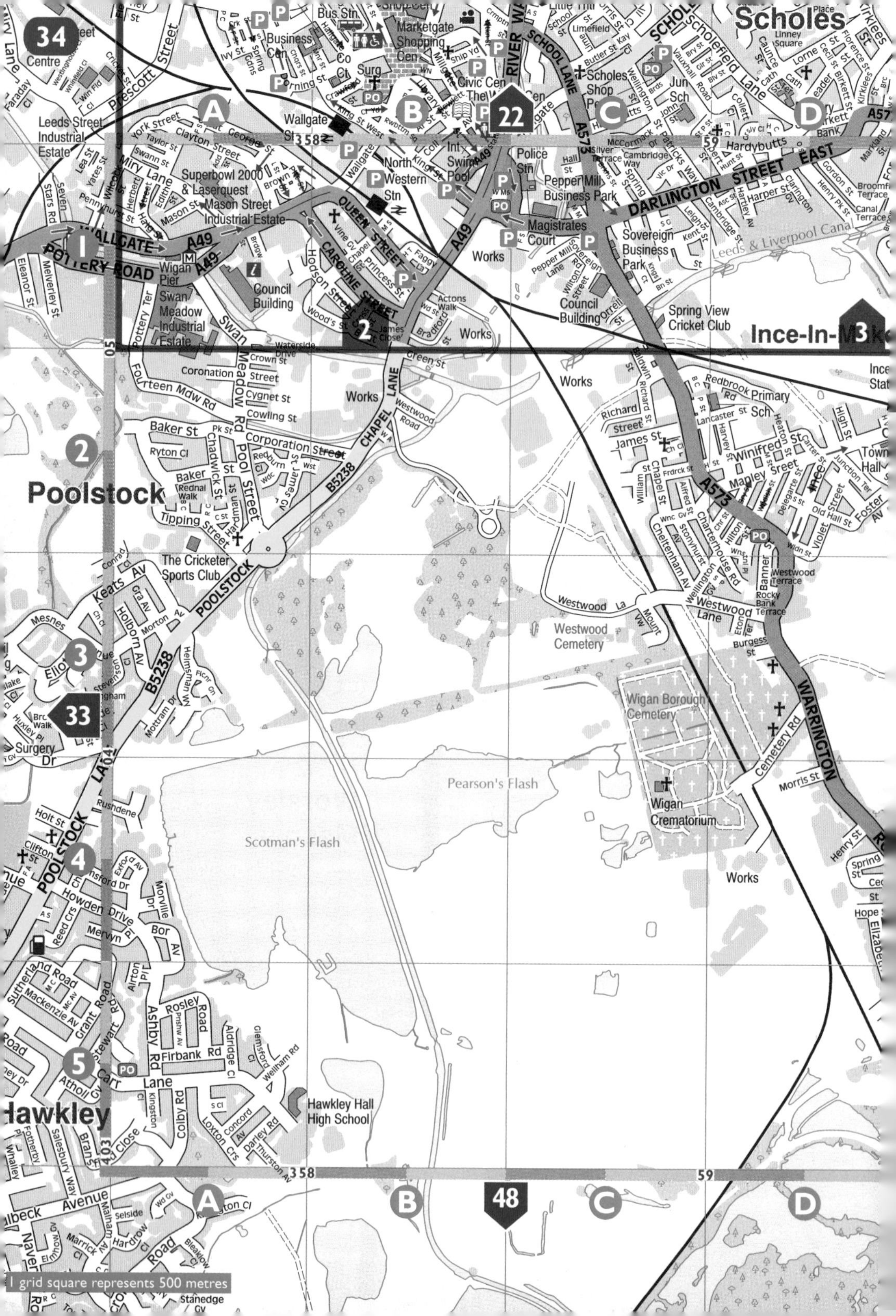

34
Centre
Leeds Street Industrial Estate
Prescott Street
Bus Stn
Business Cen
Marketgate Shopping Cen
Wallgate
King St West
Library
Civic Cen
North Western Stn
Int Swim Pool
Police Stn
River Way
School Lane
Scholes Shop Pct
Scholes
Scholefield Lane
Linney Square
Hardybutts
Darlington Street East
Pepper Mill Business Park
Magistrates Court
Sovereign Business Park
Leeds & Liverpool Canal
Council Building
Spring View Cricket Club
Ince-In-Makerfield
22
York Street
Clayton Street
George St
Miry Lane
Superbowl 2000 & Laserquest
Mason Street Industrial Estate
Wallgate
A49
Pottery Road
Wigan Pier
Swan Meadow Industrial Estate
Queen Street
Caroline Street
Hodson Street
Princess St
Acton Walk
Bradford St
Works
Pottery Ter
Swan Meadow Rd
Coronation Street
Fourteen Mdw Rd
Cygnet St
Cowling St
Chapel Lane
Westwood Road
Corporation Street
Baker St
Ryton Cl
Chadwick St
Pool Street
Rednal Walk
Tipping Street
Poolstock
The Cricketer Sports Club
B5238
Richard Street
James St
Redbrook Rd
Primary Sch
Winifred St
Manley Street
Town Hall
A573
Cheltenham Av
Charterhouse Rd
Westwood Terrace
Rocky Bank Terrace
Westwood Lane
Westwood La
Westwood Cemetery
Burgess St
Wigan Borough Cemetery
Warrington
Cemetery Rd
Morris St
Pearson's Flash
Wigan Crematorium
Scotman's Flash
Works
Keats Av
Holborn Av
Mesnes
33
Surgery
Poolstock
Holt St
Clifton St
Howden Drive
Mervyn Pl
Sutherland Road
Mackenzie Av
Grant Road
Stewart Rd
Ashby Rd
Rosley Road
Firbank Rd
Aldridge Cl
Carr Lane
Atholl Gv
Colby Rd
Loxton Crs
Concord Av
Darley Rd
Hawkley Hall High School
Hawkley
Salesbury Way
Avenue
Malham Av
Hardrow Cl
Road
Stanedge Gv
358
59
A
B
C
D
48
1 grid square represents 500 metres

Ince-in-Makerfield 35
Golf Club
Golf Course
Works
Hemfield Road
Belle Green Industrial Estate
Belle Green Lane
Chatham Street
Pennington Lane
Perth Av
Stirling Av
Battersby Street
De Trafford Dr
Ince Hall Avenue
Holt Street
Manchester Road
Empress Industrial Est
Ince Clinic & Community Centre
Surgery
Infant School
Primary School
School
Dobson Park Industrial Estate
Dobson Parkway
Mitchell Street
Grasmere Road
Ambleside Av
Petticoat Lane
Windermere Road
Keswick Pl
Lakes Terrace
Amberswood Close
Walmesley Dr
Brownlow Av
Makerfield Way
WN2
Common Nook
Seaman Way
Crown Street
Springfield Road
Primary School
Newman Cl
Darby Lane
Market Street Medical Centre
Cross St
Town Hall
Council Building
Maternity & Child Welfare Clinic
St Peters CE School
Kildare St
A577
A58
Trafford Road
Moorland Road
Harewood Rd
Hanover Rd
Waverley Rd
Hurst St
Abbott Street
Holt Street
Gilbert St
Aughton Street
Special School
Bleach Street
Harper St
Longton St
Balmoral Drive
Blackberry Dr
Borsdane Brook
Rockbourne Cl
Cashmore
Whitsbury Av
Dog Fool Brook
Newark Road
Leyland Street
Liverpool Road
Crompton Street
Works
Springbank Industrial Estate
Primary School
Pickthorn Close
Oakbank
Church Road
Health Centre
Langdale Grove
Rivington Av
Neville Street
Moss Lane
Primary School
Alfred St
Ingram St
Wright St
Waxham Gardens
Surgery
Walthew Lane
A573
Police Station
Moss St
Dale St
Hey St
Field St
Fir Tree Crs
School
Woodville Rd
Cumberbatch
Marlborough Avenue
Malvern Crs
Claydon Dr
Hathaway
Works
Wykeham Cl
Christopher Street
Laburnum Av
Maple Av
Pinewood Crs
Patricroft Rd
Canal St
Leaway
Anderton St
Bird Street
Keble St
George St
Dobson Park Industrial Estate
Platt Bridge
Platt Bridge Clinic
Medical Centre
Woodcock Dr
Hillcrest
Scafell Grove
Fieldway
Southfield
Lomax St
Ribble Rd
Lune Rd
Kent Av
Wyre Av
Calder Dr
Victoria St
Webster's Street
Stapleton Av
A58
23
36
49
E F G H
1 2 3 4 5
60 61
05 04 403

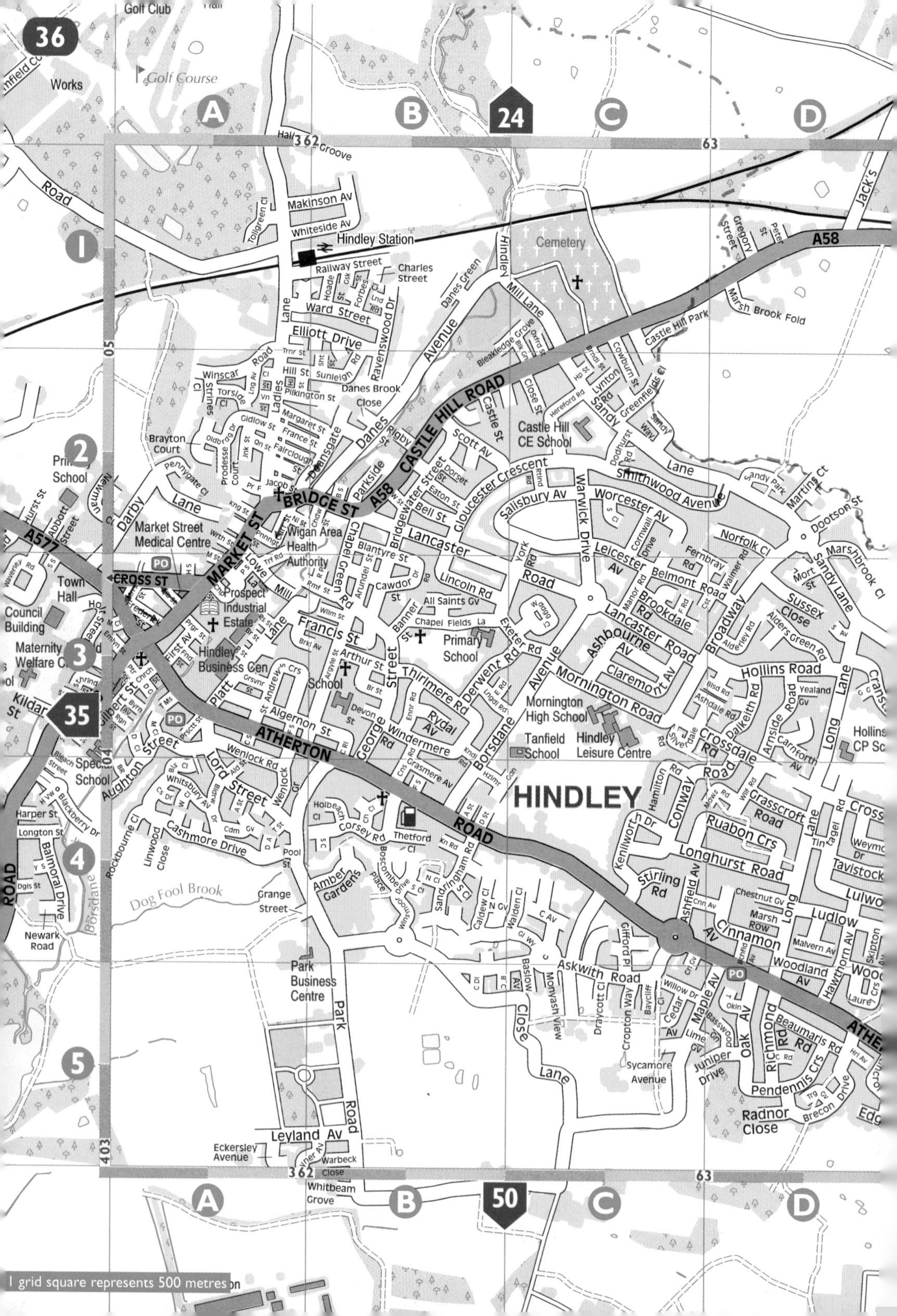

36
24
35
50
A
B
C
D
1
2
3
4
5
362
63
05
04
403
HINDLEY
Golf Club
Golf Course
Works
Hindley Station
Cemetery
Castle Hill CE School
Town Hall
Council Building
Maternity Welfare Cl
Primary School
Market Street Medical Centre
Wigan Area Health Authority
Prospect Industrial Estate
Hindley Business Cen
School
Primary School
Mornington High School
Tanfield School
Hindley Leisure Centre
Special School
Hollins CP Sc
Park Business Centre
Thetford
Dog Fool Brook
A58
A577
MARKET ST
BRIDGE ST
CASTLE HILL ROAD
ATHERTON ROAD
CROSS ST
Road
Makinson Av
Whiteside Av
Tollgreen Cl
Groove
Railway Street
Charles Street
Ward Street
Elliott Drive
Ravenswood Dr
Sunleigh Rd
Hill St
Pilkington St
Danes Brook Close
Danes Green
Avenue
Danes
Rigby
Deansgate
Ladies
Winscar
Torside Cl
Brayton Court
Gidlow St
Margaret St
France St
Fairclough St
Prodesse Court
Pennygate Cl
Darby
Lane
Newman
Abbott Street
Hurst St
Parkside
Scott Av
Castle St
Close St
Mill Lane
Bleakledge Grove
Hindley
Lynton Rd
Cowburn St
Sandy
Greenfields Cl
Sandy Way
Castle Hill Park
Marsh Brook Fold
Gregory St
Peter St
Jack's
Smithwood Avenue
Sandy Park
Martins Ct
Dootson St
Gloucester Crescent
Salisbury Av
Warwick Drive
Worcester Av
Dodhurst Rd
Bridgewater Street
Eaton St
Bell St
Lancaster
Lincoln Rd
York Rd
Road
Chapel Green Rd
Blantyre St
Arundel St
Cawdor St
All Saints Gv
Chapel Fields La
Banner St
Francis St
Arthur St
Argyle St
Andrew's Crs
Algernon St
Platt
Lane
Lowe
Mill
Leicester Av
Belmont Road
Fernbray Rd
Norfolk Cl
Marshbrook Cl
Sandy Lane
Mort St
Sussex Close
Alders Green Rd
Broadway
Brookdale Rd
Lancaster Road
Ashbourne Av
Claremont Av
Exeter Rd
Mornington Road
Hollins Road
Yealand Gv
Long Lane
Arnside Road
Carnforth Av
Dalkeith Rd
Ashdale Rd
Crossdale Rd
Road
Derwent Rd
Thirlmere Rd
Rydal Av
Windermere Rd
Grasmere Av
Borsdane Avenue
George Street
Devon St
Wenlock Rd
Lord Street
Aughton Street
Wenlock
Cashmore Drive
Linwood Close
Rockbourne Cl
Whitsbury Av
Holbeach Cl
Corsey Rd
Boscombe Place
Sandringham Rd
Amber Gardens
Winsmoor Drive
Pool St
Grange Street
Caldew Cl
Walden Cl
Askwith Road
Baslow Close
Monyash View
Draycott Cl
Cropton Way
Baycliff Cl
Clifford Pl
Stirling Rd
Kenilworth Dr
Hamilton Rd
Conway Road
Ruabon Crs
Grasscroft Road
Longhurst Road
Lane
Tintagel
Ashfield Av
Chestnut Gv
Marsh Row
Long
Cinnamon Av
Ludlow
Malvern Av
Woodland Av
Hawthorn Av
Skipton
Tavistock
Lulwo
Weymo Dr
Cedar Av
Maple Av
Willow Dr
Lime Gv
Oak Av
Richmond Rd
Beaumaris Rd
Juniper Drive
Pendennis Crs
Brecon Drive
Radnor Close
Sycamore Avenue
Lane
Close
Park Road
Leyland Av
Eckersley Avenue
Warbeck Close
Whitbeam Grove
Kildare St
Gilbert St
Harper St
Longton St
Balmoral Drive
Blackberry Dr
Bleach Street
Borsdane
Newark Road
Waverley Rd
Holt Street
First Av
Emlyn St
Frederick St
1 grid square represents 500 metres

WESTHOUGHTON
Hindley 37
CRICKETERS WAY
Police Station
Westhoughton Cricket Club
The Grange
Old
25
E
F
G
H
I
Meadows
Templeton Cl
Poplar Grove
Coverdale Rd
64
65
A58
Broad Walk
Thorn Well
Clough Avenue
Hollin
Acre
Rosebery St
Ryelands
Southfield Drive
Hawthorn Rd
Primary School
Washacre
Birch Avenue
Furze Av
Hazel Av
Chestnut Drive
Ivy Rd
Townsfield
Road
Elm Rd
The Crescent
Oxlea Gv
Greenfold Lane
Southfield Drive
Lower Southfield
Ash Gv
Pine Gv
WIGAN ROAD
Dobb Brow Road
Green
Allenby Gv
Quakerfields
Hewlett Street
Hart St
AN ROAD
PO
Fold Road
Old
Hart Common
Works
Hart Common Golf Club
Golf Course
Cunningham Road
Oakhurst Gv
Horkers Nook
School
The Pewfist
Rayden Crescent
Abbot Croft
Bentwo
St George's Avenue
School
Surgery
Southover
The Hoskers
Sandalwood
Charlock Av
Alderton Dr
Megfield
Gellert Pl
Gellert Rd
West Gv
Bellwood
Rosewood
Redwood
Osprey Av
Shearwater Drive
Brambling Dr
Wearish Lane
Cunningham Brook
Cornbrook Close
Highbury Close
France Street
Clive Road
Collins Lane
Louise Gdns
Woodwards Rd
Marsham Rd
Hartford Road
Hawkridge Cl
Fenwick Cl
Daisyhill Court
Fulmar Cl
Richard Gwyn Cl
Pinfold Cl
Pungle
Eatock
Parkway
Miry Lane
Littlegate
Daisy Hall Dr
Hallgate
Old Hall Lane
Cornergate
PO
Marsh Brook
Marshes Farm
Marlbrook Dr
Daisy Hill CE S
Hazeldene
The
Dunham Cl
Way
Higher Drake Mdw
Drake Hall
New Drake Gn
Wardens Bank
Sedgley Dr
Chapelstead
James Street
38
Hindley Road
Turner St
Old Vicarage
Rectory Gdns
The Cloisters
Mill Lane
Alder
Dalby Rd
Dorstone Cl
Green
Lane
Briar Cl
Road
Works
Lane
Swan
Coupland Road
Westlake Grove
Vale Works
Works
The Quadrangle Business Centre
Ormside Close
Wetheral Cl
Hindley Green
Sacred Heart RC School
Athol Crs
Avenue
Edinburgh Drive
Mersey Close
Severn Dr
Trent Dr
Taylor Road
Ashley Rd
Blair Av
Buchanan Lr
Stuart Av
Calder Av
Launceston Rd
Pembroke Road
Heath Gdns
Carr Common Rd
John St
School
ROAD
Thomas Street
St Johns CE Primary School
Poplar Grove
Organ St
PO
CORNER LANE
SMALLBROOK LANE
A577
Works
403
04
05
2
3
4
5
Camborne Drive
Colwyn Drive
51
Tiverton Av
Avenue
Minehead Av
Honiton Close
Hindley Green Secondary School
Baxton Row
Sarah St
A578
Heathlea
Glebe St
Russell St
Halesfield
Walls Street
Aylesbury Crs
Bexhill
Staplehurst Close
Maidstone Close
Hr Dr

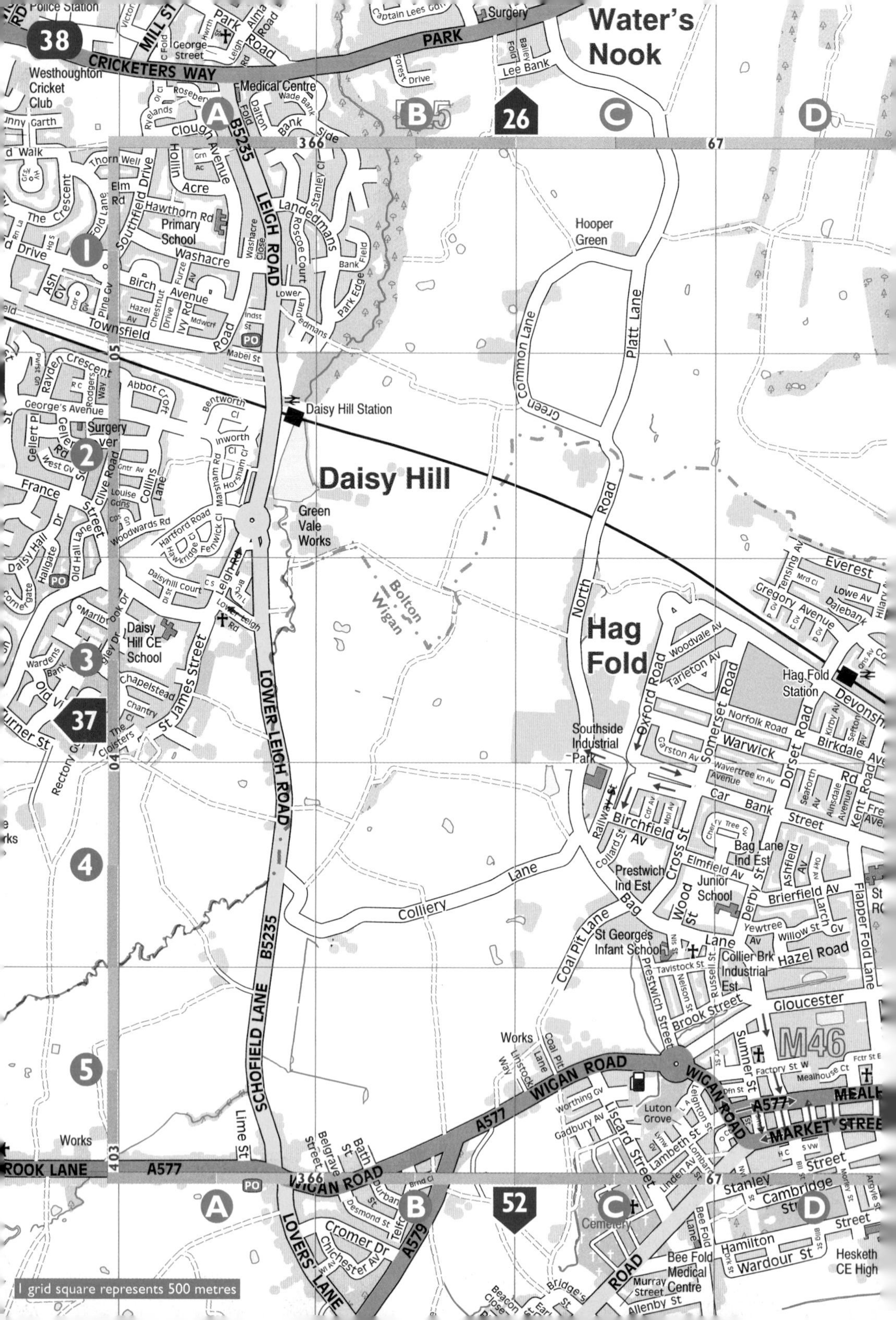

Water's Nook
Daisy Hill
Hag Fold
Westhoughton Cricket Club
Cricketers Way
Park
Leigh Road
Lower Leigh Road
Schofield Lane
B5235
Wigan Road
A577
A579
Lovers' Lane
Colliery Lane
North Road
Platt Lane
Green Common Lane
Hooper Green
Daisy Hill Station
Hag Fold Station
Green Vale Works
Southside Industrial Park
Prestwich Ind Est
Bag Lane Ind Est
Collier Brk Industrial Est
Hawthorn Rd Primary School
Daisy Hill CE School
Junior School
St George's Infant School
Bee Fold Medical Centre
Hesketh CE High
Medical Centre
Surgery
Cemetery
Works
Luton Grove
Bolton Wigan
Townsfield Road
Washacre
Landedmans
Oxford Road
Somerset Road
Dorset Road
Warwick
Norfolk Road
Car Bank Street
Birchfield Av
Cross St
Wood St
Derby St
Coal Pit Lane
Bag Lane
Hazel Road
Gloucester
Brook Street
Market Street
Cambridge St
Hamilton
Wardour St
Everest
Gregory Avenue
Devonshire
Flapper Fold Lane
Rook Lane
Cromer Dr
Chichester Av
St James Street
Chapelstead
Rectory
Turner St
Lime St
Belgrave Street
M46
38
37
26
52
A
B
C
D
1
2
3
4
5
366
367
403
404
405
1 grid square represents 500 metres

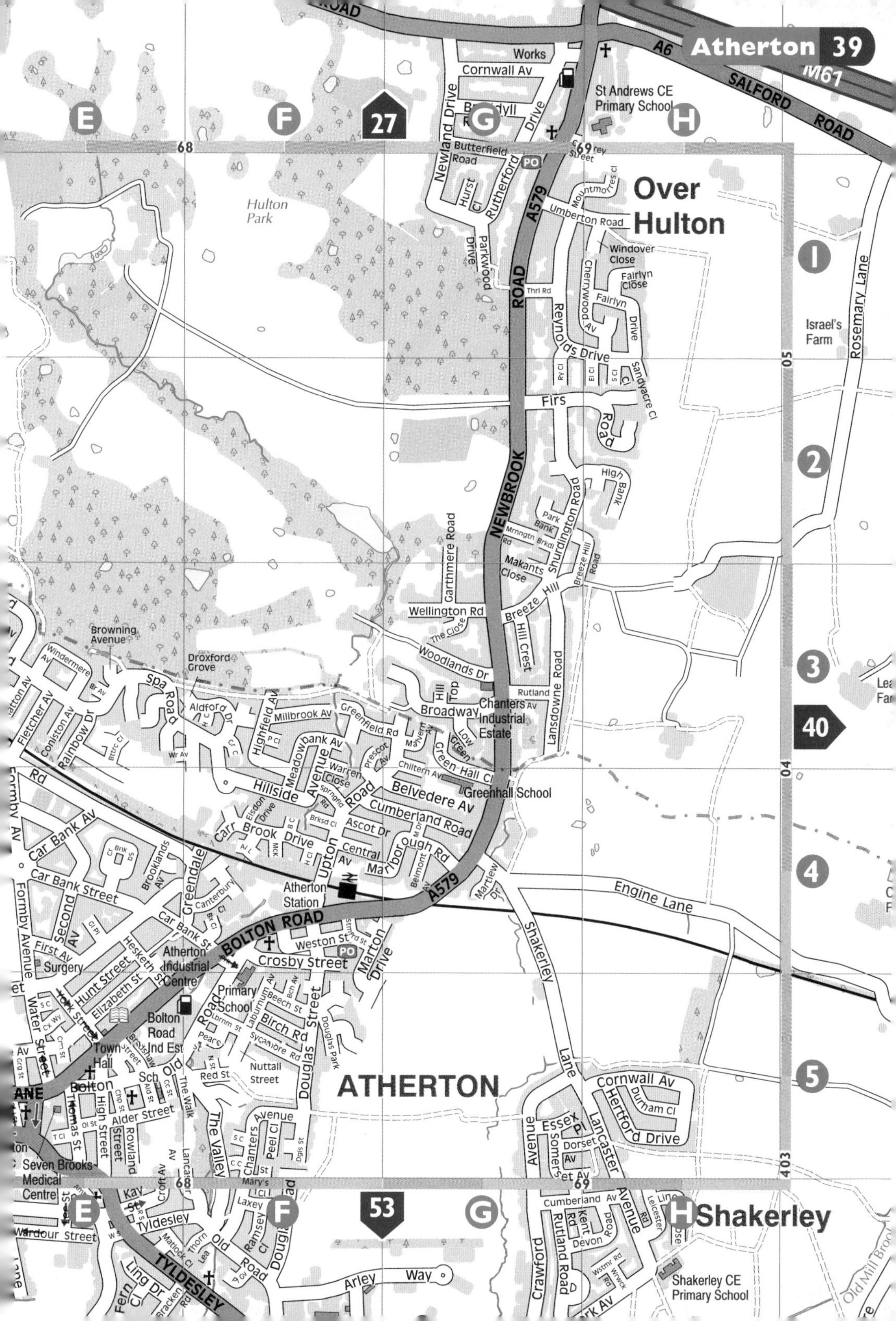

Atherton 39
A6
M61
SALFORD ROAD
Works
Cornwall Av
St Andrews CE
Primary School
E
F
27
G
H
Newland Drive
Butterfield
Road
Rutherford
PO
Hurst
Cl
Over
Hulton
Hulton
Park
A579
Umberton Road
Windover
Close
Fairlyn
Close
Fairlyn
Drive
Cherrywood Av
Parkwood
Drive
ROAD
Thrl Rd
Reynolds Drive
Israel's
Farm
Rosemary Lane
Sandyacre Cl
Firs
Road
I
2
High
Bank
NEWBROOK
Garthmere Road
Park
Bank
Shurdington Road
Breeze Hill
Road
Makants
Close
Breeze
Hill
Wellington Rd
The Close
Hill Crest
Lansdowne Road
Woodlands Dr
Rutland
Av
Browning
Avenue
Windermere
Av
Droxford
Grove
Spa
Road
Aldford
Dr
Highfield Av
Millbrook Av
Greenfield Rd
Hill
Top
Broadway
Chanters
Industrial
Estate
3
40
Fletcher Av
Coniston Av
Rainbow Dr
Meadowbank Av
Prescot
Av
Warren
Close
Low
Green
Green Hall Cl
Chiltern Av
Greenhall School
Formby
Rd
Av
Hillside
Avenue
Road
Belvedere Av
Cumberland Road
Car Bank Av
Carr
Brook
Drive
Ascot Dr
Central
Av
Upton
Marlborough Rd
Belmont
Av
Brooklands
Av
Greendale
Car Bank Street
Atherton
Station
A579
Martlew
Dr
Engine Lane
4
Formby Avenue
Second
Av
Canterbury
Cl
Car Bank St
BOLTON ROAD
Weston St
PO
Marton
Drive
Shakerley
First Av
Surgery
Hesketh St
Atherton
Industrial
Centre
Crosby Street
Hunt Street
Elizabeth St
Primary
School
Laburnum Av
Beech St
Water Street
York Street
Bolton
Road
Ind Est
Birch Rd
Street
Douglas
Sycamore Rd
Douglas Park
Town
Hall
Old
The Walk
Red St
Nuttall
Street
Lane
5
Bolton
Sch
ATHERTON
Cornwall Av
Durham Cl
Hertford Drive
Thomas St
High Street
Alder Street
Rowland
Street
Chanters Avenue
Peel Cl
The Valley
Avenue
Essex
Pl
Somerset Av
Dorset
Av
Lancaster
Seven Brooks
Medical
Centre
Lancaster
Croft Av
68
69
403
05
04
Kay
St
Laxey
Mary's
53
Cumberland Av
Kent
Rd
Avenue
Leicester
Shakerley
Tyldesley
Wardour Street
Matlock Cl
Thorn
Lea
Old
Road
Ramsey
Cl
Douglas
Rutland Road
Devon Road
Crawford
Arley
Way
TYLDESLEY
Ling Dr
Fern
Cl
Shakerley CE
Primary School
Old Mill Brook

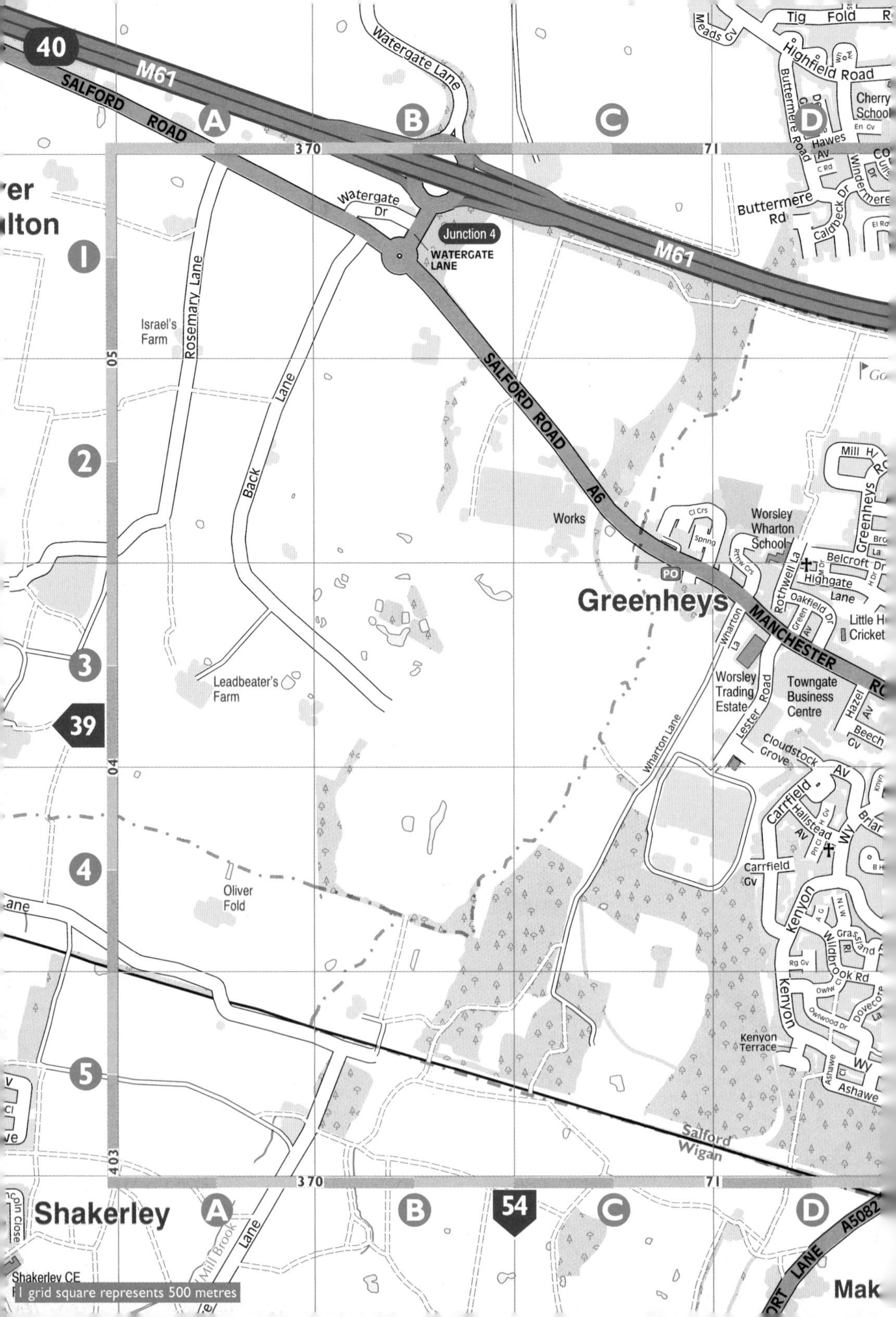

40
M61
SALFORD ROAD
Watergate Lane
Tig Fold
Meads Gv
Highfield Road
Buttermere Road
Cherry School
Hawes Av
A
B
C
D
370
71
Watergate Dr
Junction 4
WATERGATE LANE
Buttermere Rd
Caldbeck Dr
Windermere
M61
I
Israel's Farm
Rosemary Lane
05
Back Lane
SALFORD ROAD
A6
2
Works
Mill H
Greenheys
Worsley Wharton School
Rothwell La
Belcroft Dr
Highgate Lane
Oakfield Dr
PO
Greenheys
MANCHESTER
Little H
Cricket
Wharton La
3
Leadbeater's Farm
Worsley Trading Estate
Lester Road
Towngate Business Centre
Hazel Av
Beech Gv
39
Cloudstock Grove
Av
04
Wharton Lane
Carrfield
Hallstead Av
Wy
Briar
4
Oliver Fold
Carrfield Gv
Kenyon
Grassland
Wildbrook Rd
Kenyon
Dovecote
Owlwood Dr
Kenyon Terrace
Ashawe
Wy
5
Salford Wigan
403
370
71
Shakerley
A
B
54
C
D
A5082
Lane
Mill Brook
Shakerley CE
Mak
1 grid square represents 500 metres

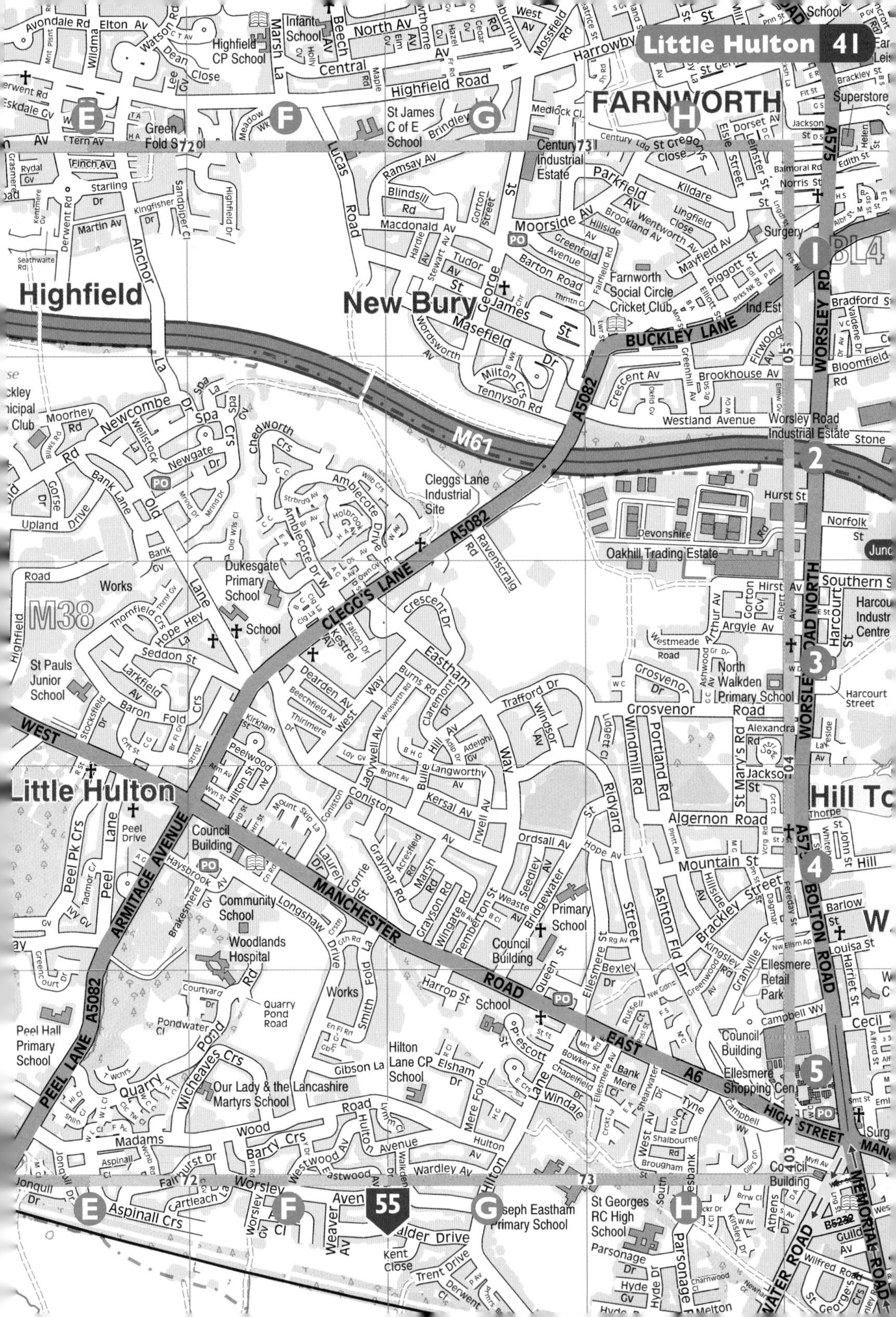

FARNWORTH
Highfield
New Bury
Little Hulton
Hill Top
M61
M38
A5082
A575
A6
B5232
BL4
CLEGG'S LANE
MANCHESTER ROAD
EAST
HIGH STREET
WORSLEY ROAD NORTH
BOLTON ROAD
MEMORIAL ROAD
PEEL LANE
ARMITAGE AVENUE
BUCKLEY LANE
WORSLEY RD
WEST
Highfield Road
Highfield CP School
St James C of E School
Century Industrial Estate
Farnworth Social Circle Cricket Club
Cleggs Lane Industrial Site
Oakhill Trading Estate
Worsley Road Industrial Estate
Dukesgate Primary School
St Pauls Junior School
North Walkden Primary School
Council Building
Community School
Woodlands Hospital
Quarry Pond Road
Peel Hall Primary School
Our Lady & the Lancashire Martyrs School
Hilton Lane CP School
St Georges RC High School
Ellesmere Retail Park
Ellesmere Shopping Centre
Superstore
Surgery
Works
Harcourt Industrial Centre
Harcourt Street
Kent Close
Parsonage
Hyde Dr
Wood Road
Madams
Aspinall Crs
Worsley
Weaver Av
Hulton Avenue
Wardley Av
Calder Drive
Trent Drive
Westland Avenue
Brookhouse Av
Crescent Av
Masefield Dr
Tennyson Rd
Wordsworth Av
Moorside Av
Barton Road
Macdonald Av
Lucas Road
Anchor La
Newcombe Dr
Bank Lane
Old Bank
Upland Drive
Gorse Dr
Moorhey Rd
Chedworth Crs
Amblecote Drive
Crescent Dr
Eastham Way
Ridyard St
Windmill Rd
Portland Rd
Grosvenor Road
Algernon Road
Mountain St
Brackley Street
Ashton Fld Dr
Ellesmere St
Queen St
Bridgewater St
Pemberton St
Wingate Rd
Grayson Rd
Coniston Av
Kersal Av
Langworthy Av
Smith Fold La
Harrop St
Prescott Lane
Windale
Hulton Av
Mere Fold
Gibson La
Wicheaves Crs
Quarry
Barry Crs
Westwood Av
Fairhurst Dr
Jonquil Dr
Cartleach La
Highfield Road
Seddon St
Hope Hey La
Larkfield Av
Baron Fold
Stocksfield Dr
Peel Pk Crs
Peel Drive
Haysbrook Av
Longshaw
Brakesmere Gv
Courtyard Dr
Pondwater Cl
Hilton St
Peelwood Av
Dearden Av
West Way
Burns Rd
Claremont Dr
Trafford Dr
Windsor Av
Ordsall Av
Hope Av
Seedley Av
Bexley Dr
Russell Ct
Bank Mere Cl
Tyne Ct
Shalbourne Rd
Brougham
Westbank
St Mary's Rd
Jackson St
Alexandra Rd
Hirst Av
Argyle Av
Westmeade Road
Arthur Av
Southern St
Hurst St
Norfolk St
Devonshire Rd
Ravenscraig Rd
Stone
Bloomfield Rd
Bradford St
Parkfield Av
Kildare
Lingfield Close
Mayfield Av
Piggott St
Greenfold Avenue
Tudor Av
Stewart Av
Blindsill Rd
Ramsay Av
Gorton Street
Harrowby St
Central Av
North Av
Elton Av
Avondale Rd
Marsh La
Infant School
Medlock Cl
St Gregory's Close
Elsie Street
Leinster St
Dorset Av
School
Green Fold School
Tern Av
Finch Av
Starling Dr
Martin Av
Derwent Rd
Kingfisher Dr
Sandpiper Cl
Louisa St
Barlow St
Harriet St
Cecil St
Campbell Wy
Kingsley Av
Granville St
Dagmar
Fereday St
Thorpe St
John St
Hill St
Athens Dr
Guild Av
Wilfred Road
St George's Crs
Memorial Road
Parsonage Dr
Joseph Eastham Primary School
Mere Fold
Elsham Dr

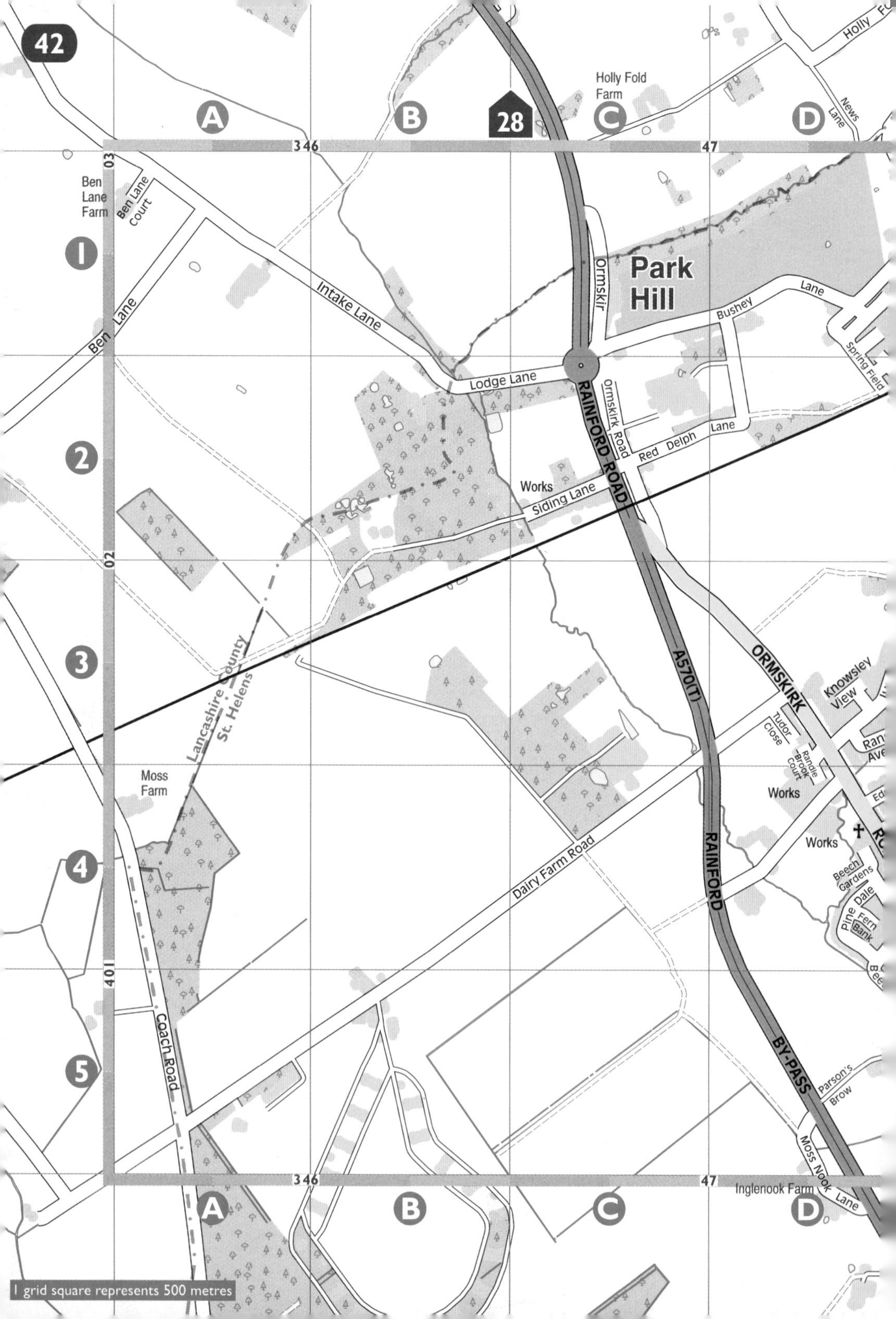

42
28
A
B
C
D
346
47
03
02
401
1
2
3
4
5
Holly Fold Farm
News Lane
Ben Lane Farm
Ben Lane Court
Ben Lane
Intake Lane
Park Hill
Bushey Lane
Spring Field
Lodge Lane
Ormskirk Road
Red Delph Lane
Works
Siding Lane
RAINFORD ROAD
A570(T)
ORMSKIRK
Knowsley View
Tudor Close
Randle Brook Court
Works
Works
Lancashire County
St. Helens
Moss Farm
Dairy Farm Road
RAINFORD
BY-PASS
Beech Gardens
Pine Dale
Fern Bank
Parson's Brow
Moss Nook Lane
Inglenook Farm
Coach Road
A
B
C
D
346
47
1 grid square represents 500 metres

Rainford Junction
Crawford
RAINFORD
News Lane
Windermere Drive
Rail Close
Kendal
Rainford Station
PO
Nook Road
Works
Maggots
Henderson Drive
Reeds Brow
Langwood Lane
Crawford Rd
Hyde's Brow
Rainford High School
Graysons Road
Brook Lodge Primary School
Harrison Drive
Helen Bank Dr
Rufford Road
Witton Way
Higher Lane
Old Lane
Avenue
Parklands
Lathom Drive
Scarisbrick Road
Duxbury Close
Standish Drive
Garswood Av
Corpus Christi RC Primary School
Holiday Moss
Victoria St
Arnian Road
Arnian Wy
The Spinney
Croxteth Drive
Muncaster Drive
Old Hall Gdns
Heyes Avenue
Heyes Grove
B5203
B5205
CROSS PIT LANE
Rainford CE Primary School
Rainford Health Centre
Gardens
Ash Grove
The Avenue
CHURCH ROAD
Leyland Road
Pilkington Street
Lakeside Gardens
Lakeside Court
Kenway
Sandon Grove
Council Building
The Kenneth Macrae Medical Centre
Southern's Lane
Eagle Crescent
HIGHER LANE
Rookery
Heron Gv
Fire Clay Farm
BOROUGH ROAD
Church Road
Holly Crs
Festival Road
Walmesley Drive
Carter Avenue
Green Lane
Thickwood Moss Lane
E
F
G
H
1
2
3
4
5
48
49
03
02
401
LC


29
44
56

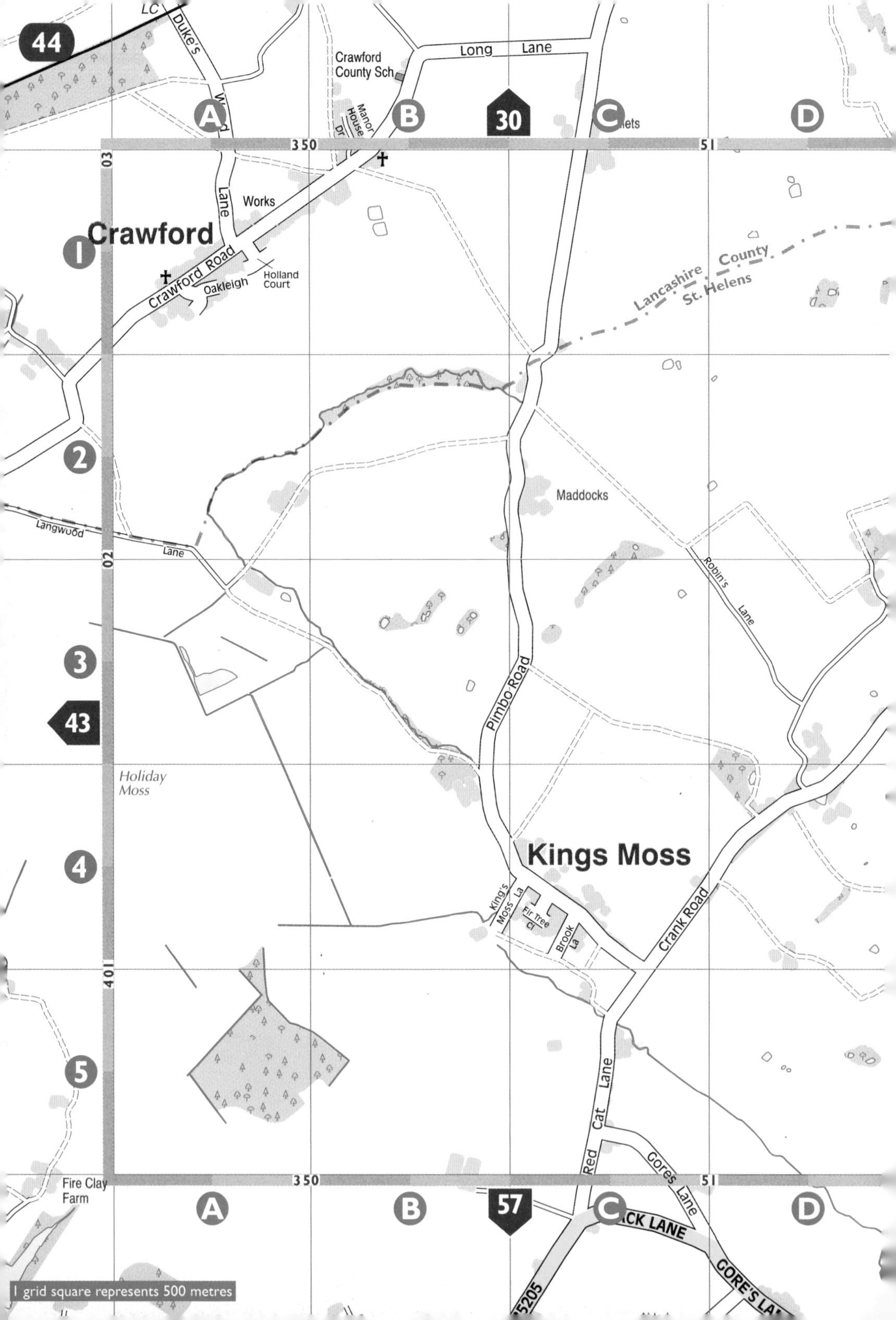
44
LC
Duke's
Ward
Lane
Crawford
County Sch
Manor
House
Dr
Long Lane
30
A
B
C
D
350
51
03
Works
Crawford
1
Crawford Road
Oakleigh
Holland
Court
Lancashire County
St. Helens
2
Langwood
Lane
Maddocks
02
Robin's
Lane
3
Pimbo Road
43
Holiday
Moss
4
Kings Moss
King's
Moss La
Fir Tree
Cl
Brook
La
Crank Road
401
5
Red Cat Lane
Gores Lane
Fire Clay
Farm
57
CK LANE
GORE'S LA
1 grid square represents 500 metres

Higher End
31
Cross La
Green La
Moss
Belmont Av
The Av
Greenslate Ct
Lakeside Av
College
Tracks Lane
Greenways
Smethurst Road
Bispham Hall Business Park
Smethurst Pk Hall
Gategill Gv
UPHOLLAND ROAD
Billinge Hospital
Coppice Dr
Crank Road
Banbury Rd
Winchester Rd
Cheltenham Dr
Coleridge Rd
Burns Close
Keats Av
Milton Gv
Tennyson Drive
Wordsworth Av
Cb Mr Av
Cob Moor Rd
B5206
Longshaw
Park Road
Longshaw Rd
Bv Av
Old
Park Av
Norfolk Rd
Longshaw Avenue
L Cl
PO
Trevelyan Dr
Wallbrook Av
Dalecrest
Brownlow La
Brownlow
Longshaw Common
Hunters Cha
Paignton Cl
Tr Dr
46
Houghwood Golf Club
Golf Course
Houghwood
Oakley Av
Beacon Road
Coultshead Av
St Aidan's Cl
A571
Red Barn Road
Ash Gv Crs
Crookhurst Av
Norbury Av
Wells
Ross Cl
Stuart Crs
MAIN STREET
Clemont Rd
London Flds
Conway Crs
Conway Dr
NEWTON
Maple Cl
Larch Close
Elm Drive
School Brow
Council Building
Royden Crs
Royden Road
Greenhill Crs
Greenhill Rd
Windsor Road
St Aidans CE Primary School
School Dr
Health Cen
Blackleyhurst
Andrew Av
Gorsey Brow
Well Wy
Robys
ROAD
BILL
58
52
53
03
02
01
E
F
G
H
I
2
3
4
5

46
Winstanley College
Winsta
32
A
B
C
D
354
55
Winstanley Road
Park Road
M6
A571
PEMBERTON ROAD
Springpool
New Houses
Pine View
Sycamore Dr
Beech Walk
Sunnyfields
Tan House La
Mendip
Malvern Cl
Pennine Av
Cleveland
Cheviot Cl
Cambrian Crs
School
Wirral Dr
Coleshill Ri
Shefford Crs
Castleton Way
Chelmorton Gv
Elkstone Cl
Burley Cl
Bratton
Sykes Crs
Paris Av
Banham Av
Norfolk Rd
Longshaw Avenue
Longshaw Common
45
WIGAN ROAD
Works
Ashton Road
Maddox Farm
Winstanley Road
Wigan
St. Helens
Coultshead Av
St Aidan's Cl
NEWTON ROAD
B5207
BILLINGE ROAD
59
Conway Crs
Conway Dr
Royden Crs
Royden Road
Greenhill Crs
Greenhill Rd
Windsor Road
Claremont Rd
London Flds
St Aidans CE Primary School
BILLINGE
Garswood United FC
Leyland
Downall Green
1 grid square represents 500 metres

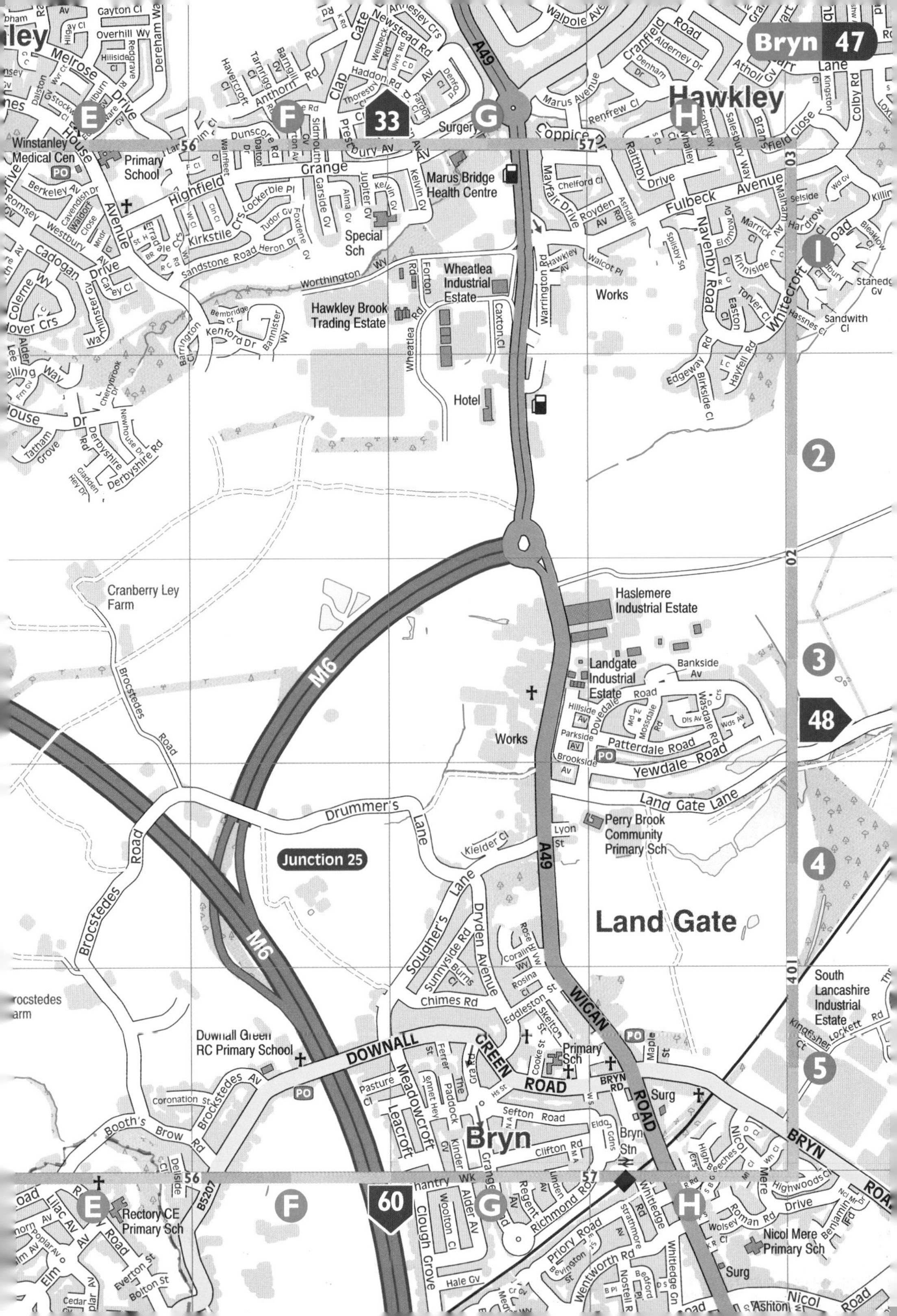

Bryn 47
Hawkley
Land Gate
Bryn
Junction 25
A49
M6
WIGAN ROAD
DOWNALL GREEN ROAD
BRYN ROAD
Winstanley Medical Cen
Primary School
Marus Bridge Health Centre
Special Sch
Wheatlea Industrial Estate
Hawkley Brook Trading Estate
Works
Hotel
Surgery
Haslemere Industrial Estate
Landgate Industrial Estate
Perry Brook Community Primary Sch
Cranberry Ley Farm
Downall Green RC Primary School
Rectory CE Primary Sch
Nicol Mere Primary Sch
South Lancashire Industrial Estate
Bryn Stn
Surg
Melrose Drive
Highfield Grange Av
Sandstone Road
Worthington Wy
Kenford Dr
Cadogan Drive
Westbury Av
Berkeley Av
Romsey
Colerne Wy
Dover Crs
Tatham Grove
Derbyshire Rd
Newhouse Dr
Cherrybrook Dr
Gayton Cl
Overhill Wy
Dereham Wy
Anthorn Rd
Haddon Rd
Newstead Rd
Prestbury Av
Sidmouth Gv
Kelvin Gv
Jupiter Gv
Garside Gv
Walpole Av
Cranfield Road
Marus Avenue
Renfrew Cl
Coppice Dr
Mayfair Drive
Royden Av
Raithby Drive
Fulbeck Avenue
Navenby Road
Whitecroft Road
Warrington Rd
Caxton Cl
Wheatlea Rd
Forton Rd
Brocstedes Road
Drummer's Lane
Land Gate Lane
Yewdale Road
Patterdale Road
Dovedale Road
Bankside Av
Sougher's Lane
Dryden Avenue
Sunnyside Rd
Chimes Rd
Eddleston St
Sefton Road
Clifton Rd
Meadowcroft
Leacroft
Clough Grove
Alder Av
Woolton Cl
Richmond Rd
Priory Road
Wentworth Rd
Whitledge Rd
Roman Rd
Nicol Road
Booth's Brow Rd
Brockstedes Av
Coronation St
Lilac Av
Everton St
Bolton St
Highwoods Cl
Mere Drive
Kingfisher Ct
Lockett Rd
Sandwith Cl
Stanedge Gv

48
Hawkley
Carr Lane
Firbank Rd
Aldridge Cl
Colby Rd
Hawkley Hall High School
Bransfield Close
Salesbury Way
Avenue
Navenby Road
Malham Av
Selside
Killington Cl
Hardrow
Whitecroft Road
Bleaklow
Stanedge Gv
Sandwith Cl
Hassnes Cl
Torver Cl
Easton
Hayfell Rd
Birkside Cl
34
A
B
C
D
358
59
1
2
3
4
5
03
02
01
Leeds & Liverpool Canal
Park House Farm
Bryn Gates Lane
Bankside Av
Wasdale Rd
47
Road
Gate Lane
Three Sisters
Three Sisters Rd
South Lancashire Industrial Estate
Kingfisher Ct
Lockett Rd
Antler Ct
Lockett Road
Kestrel Dr
Redgate Rd
Beaver Ct
Ashton Grange Industrial Estate
Hall
James St
A58
BOLTON ROAD
BRYN
Highwoods Cl
Mere Drive
Roman Rd
Nicol Mere Primary Sch
B5207
61
Stubshaw Cross
South Lancashire Industrial Estate
Bolton Rd
Severn Road
Avon Rd
Welland Road
Conway Rd
Luke St
Hope St
School
1 grid square represents 500 metres

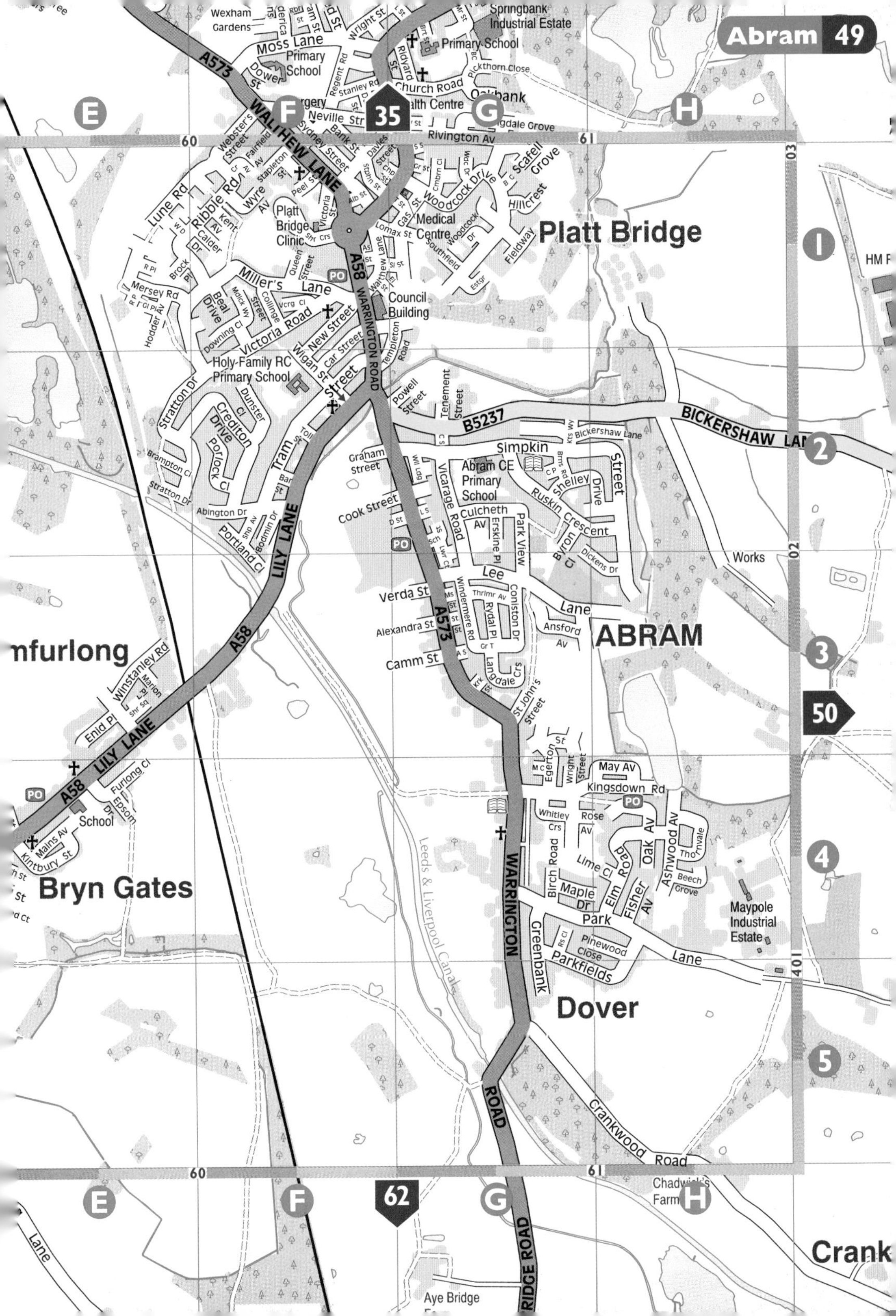
Platt Bridge
ABRAM
Bryn Gates
Dover
mfurlong
Crank
Springbank Industrial Estate
Maypole Industrial Estate
Wexham Gardens
Moss Lane
Primary School
Church Road
Oakbank
Neville St
Rivington Av
WALTHEW LANE
Webster's Street
Sydney Street
Bank St
Davies Street
Scafell Grove
Woodcock Drive
Hillcrest
Fieldway
Medical Centre
Lomax St
Southfield
Platt Bridge Clinic
Lune Rd
Ribble Rd
Wyre Av
Kent Av
Calder Dr
Brock Pl
Mersey Rd
Hodder Av
Miller's Lane
Queen Street
Council Building
Beal Drive
Collinge Street
Victoria Road
New Street
Car Street
Wigan St
Downing Cl
Holy Family RC Primary School
Templeton Road
WARRINGTON ROAD
Powell Street
Tenement Street
B5237
BICKERSHAW LANE
Bickershaw Lane
Simpkin Street
Stratton Dr
Crediton Drive
Dunster Cl
Porlock Cl
Tram Street
Brampton Cl
Stratton Dr
Abington Dr
Bodmin Dr
Portland Cl
LILY LANE
Graham Street
Vicarage Road
Abram CE Primary School
Cook Street
Culcheth Av
Erskine Pl
Park View
Shelley Drive
Ruskin Crescent
Byron Cl
Dickens Dr
Works
Lee Lane
Verda St
Windermere Rd
Rydal Pl
Coniston Dr
Alexandra St
Ansford Av
A573
Camm St
Langdale Crs
A58
Winstanley Rd
Marion Pl
Enid Pl
St John's Street
Egerton St
Wright Street
May Av
Kingsdown Rd
Furlong Cl
Epsom Dr
School
Mains Av
Kintbury St
Whitley Crs
Rose Av
Oak Av
Ashwood Av
Thornvale
Lime Cl
Elm Road
Birch Road
Maple Dr
Fisher Av
Beech Grove
Park Lane
Greenbank
Pinewood Close
Parkfields
Leeds & Liverpool Canal
Crankwood Road
Chadwick's Farm
Aye Bridge
Lane
HM P
E F G H
I 2 3 4 5
60 61
03 02 401
35 50 62

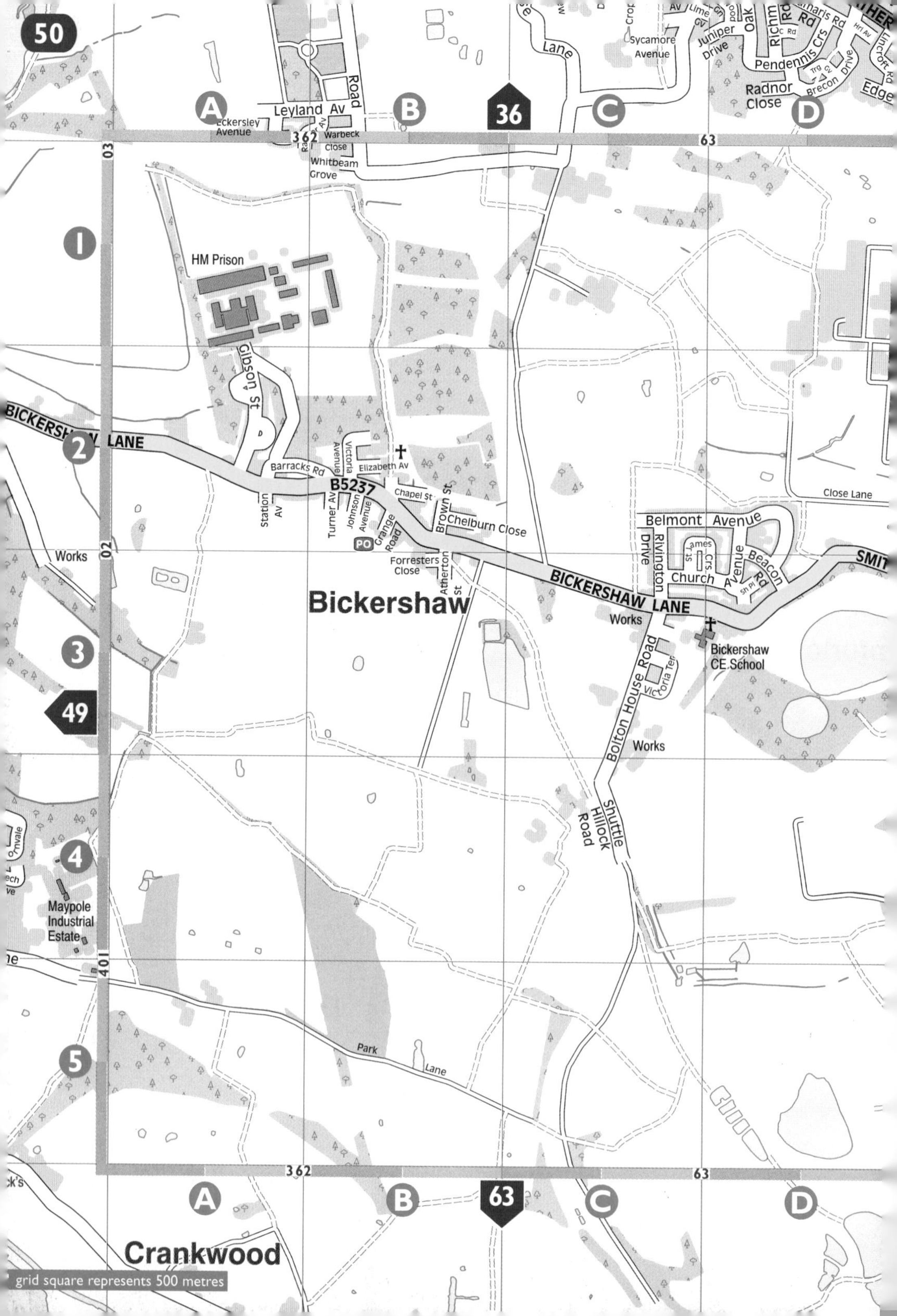

50
36
49
63
A
B
C
D
1
2
3
4
5
362
63
03
02
401
Leyland Av
Eckersley Avenue
Road
Warbeck Close
Whitbeam Grove
Lane
Sycamore Avenue
Juniper Drive
Oak
Pendennis Crs
Radnor Close
Brecon Drive
Edge
HM Prison
Gibson St
BICKERSHAW LANE
Barracks Rd
Victoria Avenue
Elizabeth Av
B5237
Chapel St
Station Av
Turner Av
Johnson Avenue
Grange Road
PO
Brown St
Chelburn Close
Forresters Close
Atherton St
Works
Bickershaw
Belmont Avenue
Rivington Drive
St James Crs
Church Avenue
Beacon Rd
Close Lane
SMIT
Works
Bickershaw CE School
Bolton House Road
Victoria Ter
Works
Shuttle Hillock Road
Maypole Industrial Estate
Park Lane
Crankwood
grid square represents 500 metres

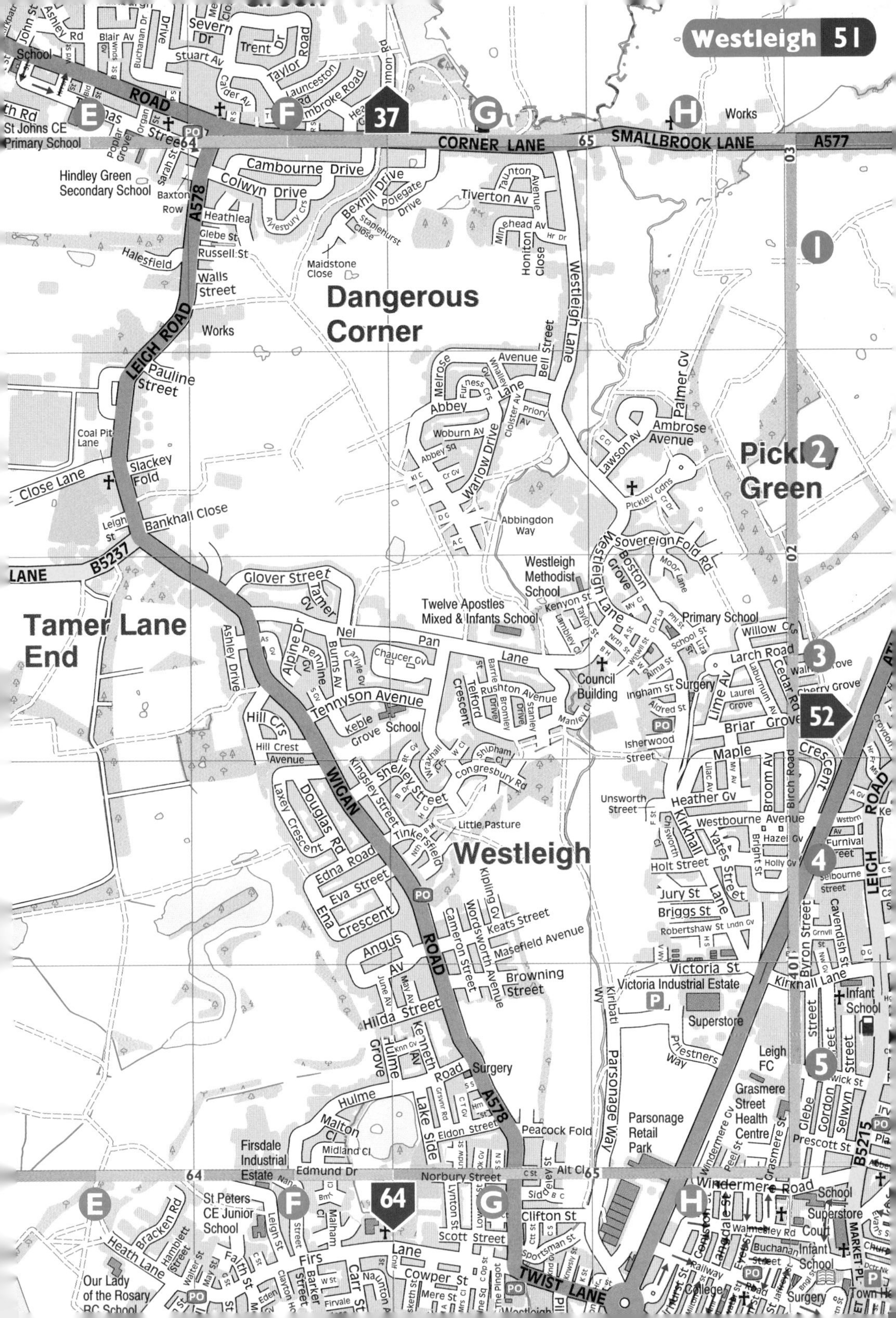
Dangerous Corner
Tamer Lane End
Westleigh
Pickley Green
CORNER LANE
SMALLBROOK LANE
A577
LEIGH ROAD
A578
WIGAN ROAD
TWIST LANE
B5237
B5215
37
52
64
St Johns CE Primary School
Hindley Green Secondary School
Works
Cambourne Drive
Colwyn Drive
Bexhill Drive
Polegate Drive
Tiverton Av
Minehead Av
Honiton Close
Maidstone Close
Staplehurst Close
Aylesbury Crs
Heathlea
Glebe St
Russell St
Halesfield
Walls Street
Baxton Row
Pauline Street
Coal Pit Lane
Slackey Fold
Close Lane
Bankhall Close
Leigh St
Westleigh Lane
Bell Street
Melrose Avenue
Abbey Lane
Woburn Av
Abbey Sq
Warlow Drive
Cloister Av
Priory Av
Abbingdon Way
Palmer Gv
Ambrose Avenue
Lawson Av
Pickley Gdns
Sovereign Fold Rd
Boston Grove
Moor Lane
Westleigh Methodist School
Twelve Apostles Mixed & Infants School
Primary School
Glover Street
Tamer Gv
Nel Pan Lane
Ashley Drive
Alpine Dr
Pennine Gv
Burns Av
Chaucer Gv
Tennyson Avenue
Keble Grove School
Hill Crs
Hill Crest Avenue
Telford Crescent
Rushton Avenue
Kenyon St
Taylor St
Council Building
Ingham St
Surgery
Alfred St
Isherwood Street
Willow Crs
Larch Road
Cedar Rd
Lime Av
Laurel Grove
Laburnum Av
Briar Grove
Maple
Crescent
Birch Road
Broom Av
Heather Gv
Westbourne Avenue
Unsworth Street
Kirkhall Lane
Yates Street
Holt Street
Jury St
Briggs St
Robertshaw St
Victoria St
Victoria Industrial Estate
Superstore
Priestners Way
Leigh FC
Kirkhall Lane
Byron Street
Cavendish St
Selbourne Street
Infant School
Shelley Street
Kingsley Street
Congresbury Rd
Little Pasture
Tinkersfield
Laxey Crescent
Douglas Rd
Edna Road
Eva Street
Ena Crescent
Angus Av
Cameron Street
Wordsworth Avenue
Kipling Gv
Keats Street
Masefield Avenue
Browning Street
Hilda Street
Hulme Grove
Kenneth Av
Hulme Road
Malton Cl
Lake Side
Eldon Street
Midland Cl
Peacock Fold
Parsonage Way
Parsonage Retail Park
Grasmere Street
Health Centre
Glebe Street
Gordon Street
Selwyn Street
Prescott St
Firsdale Industrial Estate
Edmund Dr
Norbury Street
Windermere Road
St Peters CE Junior School
Bracken Rd
Heath Lane
Hamblett Street
Faith St
Our Lady of the Rosary RC School
Firs Lane
Carr St
Cowper St
Lynton St
Scott Street
Clifton St
Sportsman St
Coniston St
Langdale St
Walmesley Rd
Buchanan Street
Railway Road
College
School
Superstore
Court
Infant School
MARKET PL
Town
Surgery

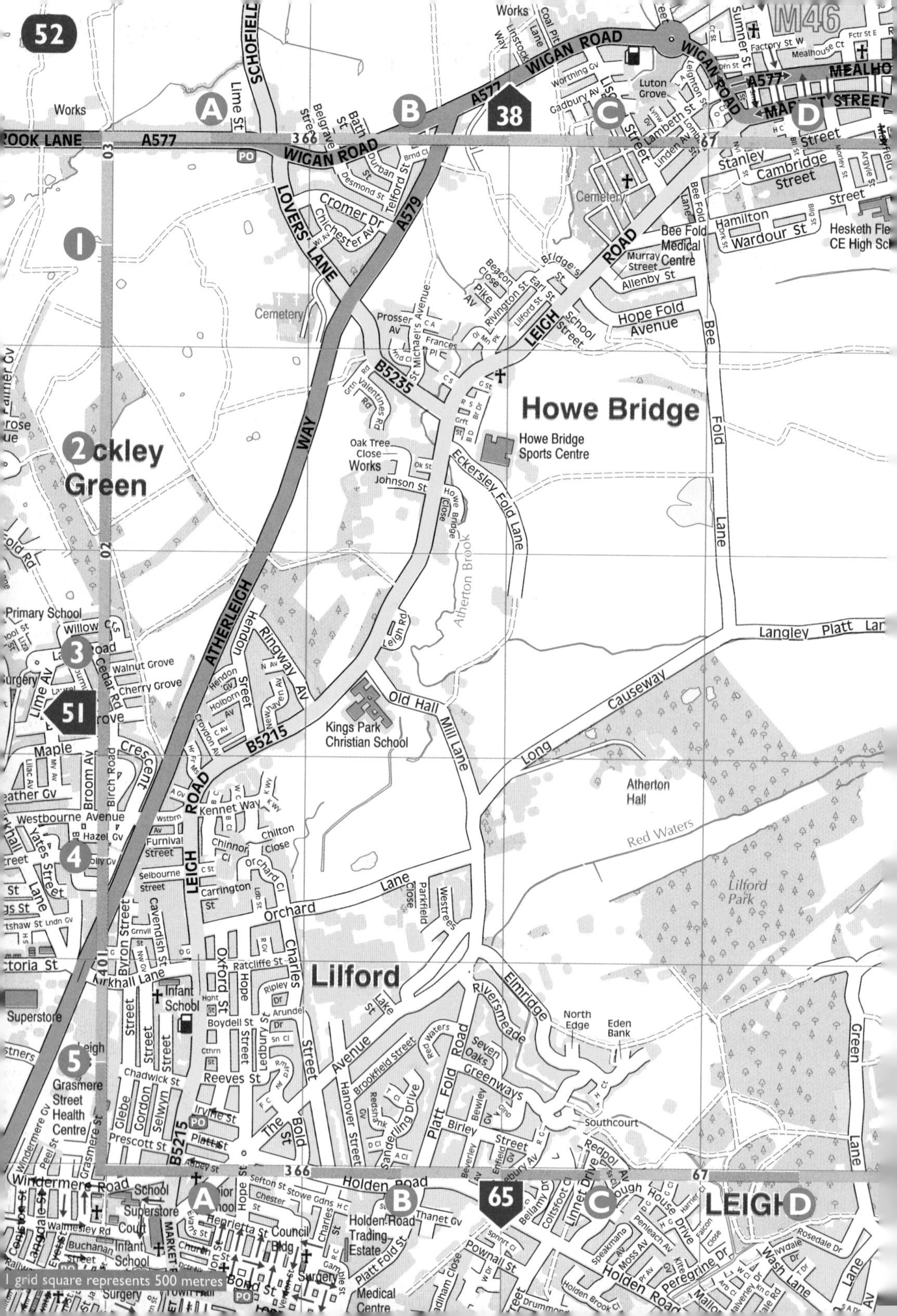
M46
Works
SCHOFIELD
Lime St
Works
ROOK LANE
A577
WIGAN ROAD
A577
38
Wigan Road
Luton Grove
Leighton St
Lambeth St
Linden Av
Worthing Gv
Gadbury Av
Sumner St
Factory St W
Mealhouse Ct
MEALHO
MARKET STREET
A577
Stanley
Cambridge Street
Street
Hamilton
Wardour St
Hesketh Fle
CE High Sc
Bee Fold Medical Centre
Murray Street
Allenby St
Hope Fold Avenue
Bee Fold Lane
Cemetery
Belgrave Street
Bath St
Durban St
Desmond St
Telford St
Cromer Dr
Chichester Av
LOVERS' LANE
A579
Cemetery
Beacon Close
Pike Av
Rivington St
Earl St
Lilford St
Bridge's St
School Street
LEIGH ROAD
Prosser Av
St Michael's Avenue
Frances Pl
B5235
Valentines Rd
Howe Bridge
Howe Bridge Sports Centre
Oak Tree Close
Works
Johnson St
Eckersley Fold Lane
Howe Bridge Close
Atherton Brook
ATHERLEIGH WAY
Leigh Rd
Langley Platt Lane
Causeway
Long
Atherton Hall
Red Waters
Lilford Park
Old Hall Mill Lane
Kings Park Christian School
Hendon Street
Ringway Av
Newhaven Av
B5215
Croydon Av
Holborn Av
LEIGH ROAD
Kennet Way
Chilton Close
Chinnor Cl
Orchard Cl
Carrington St
Orchard Lane
Parkfield Close
Westrees
Atherton Green
Primary School
Willow Crs
Road
Lime Av
Cedar Rd
Walnut Grove
Cherry Grove
51
Surgery
Maple
Crescent
Birch Road
Broom Av
Heather Gv
Westbourne Avenue
Hazel Gv
Furnival Street
Selbourne Street
Yates Street
Lane
Byron Street
Cavendish St
Victoria St
Kirkhall Lane
Superstore
Infant School
Oxford St
Hope Street
Ratcliffe St
Charles Street
Lilford
Ripley Dr
Arundel Dr
Ledbury St
Boydell St
Reeves St
Irvine St
Platt St
Prescott St
Chadwick St
Glebe Street
Gordon Street
Selwyn Street
Grasmere Street Health Centre
Windermere Gv
Peel St
Grasmere St
B5215
Leigh
The Bold St
Hanover Street
Avenue
Lake St
Brookfield Street
Sanderling Drive
Platt Fold Road
Riversmeade
Elmridge
Seven Oaks
Greenways
Birley Street
North Edge
Eden Bank
Southcourt
Redpol Av
Linnet Drive
Coltsfoot Cl
Bellamy Dr
Green Lane
Windermere Road
School
Superstore
Court
Infant School
Buchanan Street
Walmesley Rd
Coniston St
Langdale St
Abbey St
Hope St
Sefton St
Stowe Gdns
Chester St
Holden Road
Henrietta St
Council Bldg
Holden Road Trading Estate
Thanet Gv
Platt Fold St
Church St
Bond St
Surgery
Town Hall
Medical Centre
MARKET ST
65
Pownall St
Spinnaker Cl
Holden Road
Speakman Av
Moss Av
Penleach Av
House Drive
Falcon Close
Peregrine Dr
Holden Brook Cl
LEIGH
Rosedale Dr
Wash Lane
Lane
366
67
03
02
401
1
2
3
4
5
A
B
C
D
PO
1 grid square represents 500 metres

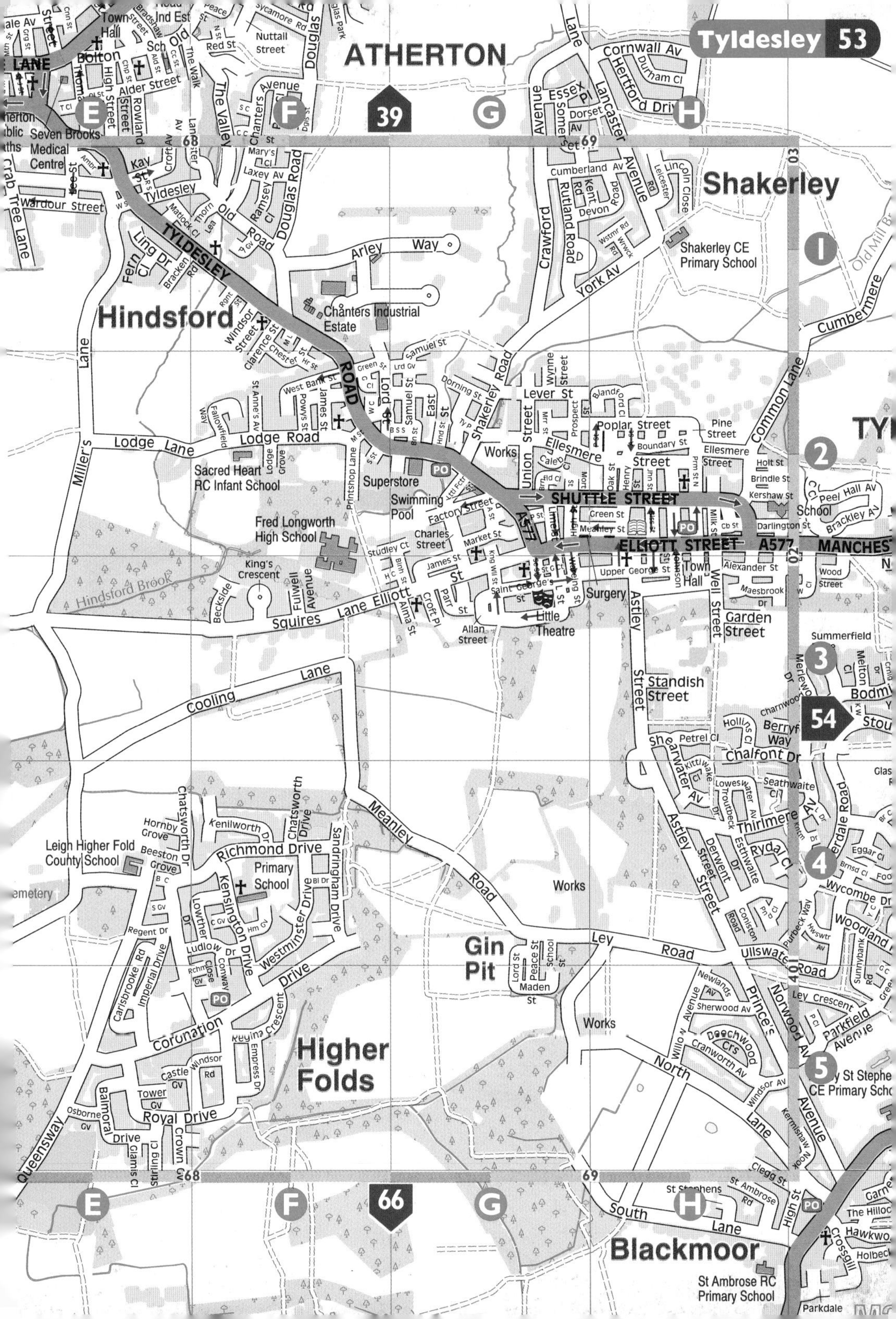
ATHERTON
39
Town Hall
Ind Est
Nuttall Street
Douglas
Bolton
High Street
Alder Street
Rowland
The Valley
The Walk
Chanters Avenue
Red St
Seven Brooks Medical Centre
Crab Tree Lane
Wardour Street
Kay St
Tyldesley
Laxey Av
Ramsey Cl
Douglas Road
Old Road
TYLDESLEY
ROAD
Ling Dr
Fern Cl
Bracken Rd
Arley Way
Chanters Industrial Estate
Hindsford
Windsor Street
Clarence St
Chester St
Samuel St
Miller's Lane
Lodge Lane
Lodge Road
Fallowfield Way
St Anne's Av
Lodge Grove
Sacred Heart RC Infant School
West Bank St
James St
Lord St
East St
Printshop Lane
Superstore
Swimming Pool
Factory Street
Fred Longworth High School
Charles Street
Studley Ct
Market St
King's Crescent
Hindsford Brook
Beckside
Fulwell Avenue
Squires Lane
Elliott St
Alma St
Croft Pl
Parr St
Allan Street
Saint George's St
Little Theatre
Surgery
Astley Street
Shakerley Road
Dorning St
Lever St
Union Street
Wynne Street
Ellesmere Street
Poplar Street
Boundary St
Pine Street
Ellesmere Street
SHUTTLE STREET
ELLIOTT STREET
A577
MANCHESTER
Green St
Upper George St
Town Hall
Well Street
Alexander St
Maesbrook Dr
Garden Street
Common Lane
Holt St
Brindle St
Kershaw St
Darlington St
Peel Hall Av
School
Brackley Av
Wood Street
Works
Shakerley
Cornwall Av
Durham Cl
Hertford Drive
Lancaster Avenue
Essex Pl
Dorset Av
Somerset
Cumberland Av
Rutland Road
Kent Rd
Devon Road
Crawford Avenue
Lincoln Close
Leicester Rd
York Av
Shakerley CE Primary School
Cumbermere
Old Mill
Summerfield
Merlewood Dr
Melton Cl
54
Charnwood
Berryfield Way
Hollins Cl
Chalfont Dr
Standish Street
Petrel Cl
Shearwater Av
Kittiwake Dr
Loweswater Av
Seathwaite Cl
Troutbeck Dr
Thirlmere Av
Esthwaite Dr
Derwent Dr
Rydal Cl
Astley Street
Eggar Cl
Wycombe Dr
Woodland
Purbeck Way
Coniston Road
Ullswater Road
Sunnybank Av
Ley Crescent
Parkfield Avenue
St Stephens CE Primary School
Norwood Av
Prince's Avenue
Cooling Lane
Meanley Road
Chatsworth Dr
Chatsworth Drive
Kenilworth Dr
Hornby Grove
Beeston Grove
Leigh Higher Fold County School
Richmond Drive
Primary School
Kensington Drive
Sandringham Drive
Westminster Drive
Lowther Dr
Regent Dr
Carisbrooke Rd
Imperial Drive
Ludlow Dr
Conway Close
Gin Pit
Lord St
Peace St
School St
Maden St
Ley Road
Works
Newlands Av
Sherwood Av
Willow Avenue
Beechwood Crs
Cranworth Av
North Lane
Windsor Av
Kermishaw Nook
Coronation Drive
Regina Crescent
Empress Dr
Windsor Rd
Castle Gv
Tower Gv
Royal Drive
Higher Folds
Osborne Gv
Balmoral Drive
Glamis Cl
Stirling Cl
Crown Gv
Queensway
Cemetery
66
Clegg St
St Stephens
St Ambrose Rd
High St
South Lane
Blackmoor
St Ambrose RC Primary School
The Hillock
Hawkwood
Holbeck
Crossgill
Parkdale
E
F
G
H
68
69
1
2
3
4
5
02
03
401

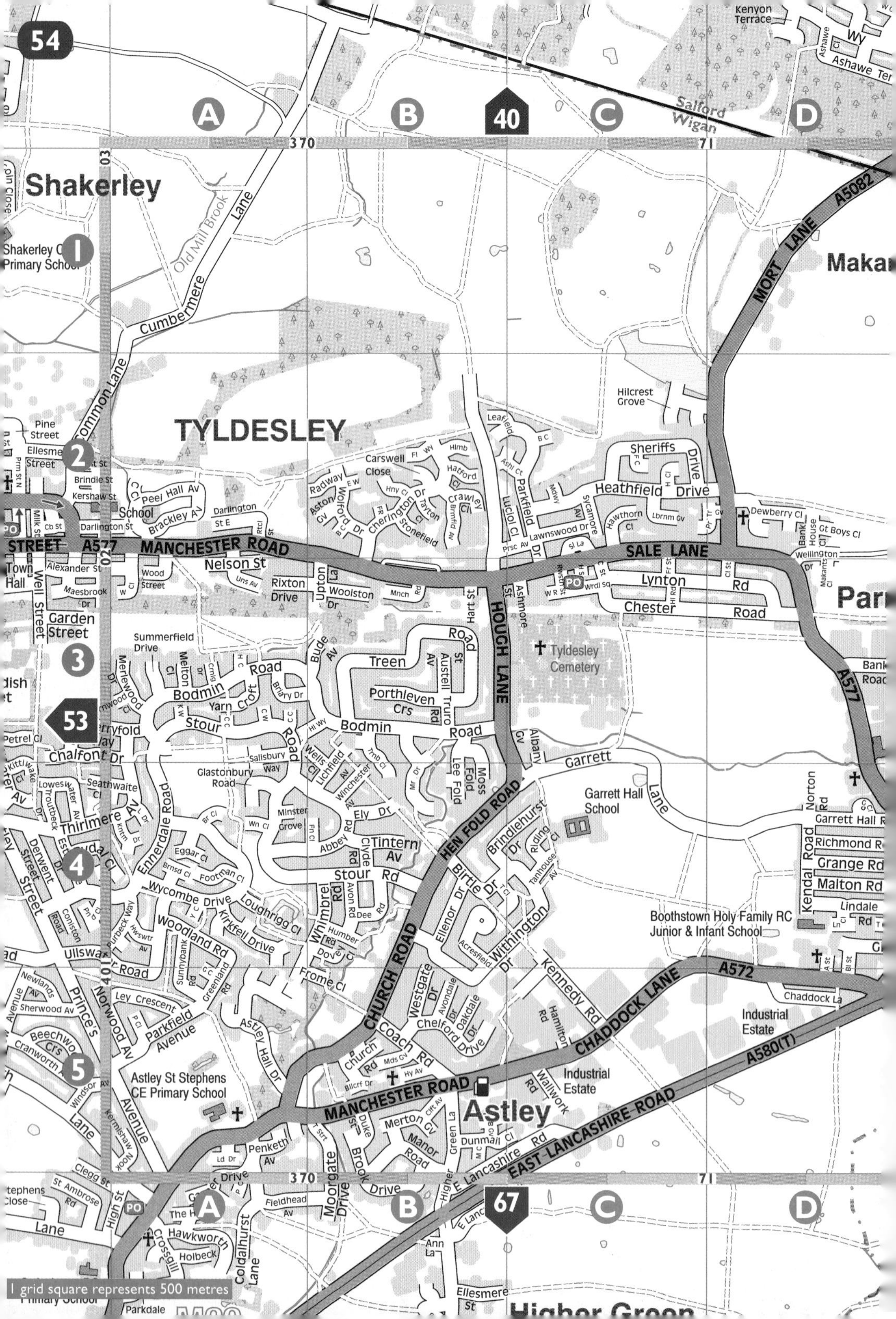
54
40
53
67
A
B
C
D
1
2
3
4
5
370
71
03
02
01
Kenyon Terrace
Ashawe Terr
Salford
Wigan
Shakerley
Shakerley CE Primary School
Old Mill Brook
Cumbermere Lane
Common Lane
TYLDESLEY
Makants
Mort Lane
A5082
Hilcrest Grove
Pine Street
Ellesmere Street
Brindle St
Kershaw St
School
Peel Hall Av
Brackley Av
Darlington St E
Darlington St
Milk St
Cb St
Carswell Close
Radway
Aston Gv
Wolford Dr
Cherington Dr
Tayton Cl
Stonefield
Hatford Cl
Crawley Cl
Brmfld Av
Leafield
Ashl Ct
Parkfield Dr
Luciol Cl
Sheriffs Drive
Heathfield Drive
Sycamore Av
Hawthorn Cl
Lbrnm Gv
Dewberry Cl
Bank House Cl
Gt Boys Cl
Wellington Dr
Makants Cl
STREET
A577
MANCHESTER ROAD
SALE LANE
Town Hall
Alexander St
Wood Street
Nelson St
Uns Av
Rixton Drive
Upton La
Woolston Dr
Mnch Rd
Hart St
HOUGH LANE
Ashmore St
Prsc Av
Lawnswood Dr
Lynton Rd
Chester Road
Wrdl Sq
PO
Parr
Well Street
Maesbrook Dr
Garden Street
Summerfield Drive
Merlewood Dr
Melton Cl
Bodmin Road
Yarn Croft
Briary Dr
Bude Av
Treen Road
Austell St
Porthleven Crs
Truro Rd
Bodmin Road
Stour Road
Tylldesley Cemetery
Bank Road
A577
Berryfold Way
Petrel Cl
Chalfont Dr
Salisbury Way
Wells Cl
Lichfield Av
Winchester Av
Mr Dr
Lee Fold
Moss Fold
Albany Gv
Garrett Lane
Glastonbury Road
Seathwaite Cl
Loweswater Av
Troutbeck Dr
Thirlmere Av
Ennerdale Road
Minster Grove
Ely Dr
Abbey Rd
Clyde Rd
Tintern Av
HEN FOLD ROAD
Brindlehurst Dr
Riding Cl
Garrett Hall School
Norton Rd
Garrett Hall Rd
Kendal Road
Richmond Rd
Grange Rd
Malton Rd
Lindale Rd
Derwent Street
Rydal Cl
Eggar Cl
Footman Cl
Stour Rd
Whimbrel Rd
Avon Rd
Dee Rd
Birtle Dr
Ellenor Dr
Tanhouse Av
Wycombe Drive
Loughrigg Cl
Kirkfell Drive
Humber Rd
Dovey Cl
Acresfield
Withington Dr
Boothstown Holy Family RC Junior & Infant School
Coniston Road
Purbeck Way
Woodland Rd
Sunnybank Rd
Greenland Rd
Frome Cl
CHURCH ROAD
Kennedy Rd
CHADDOCK LANE
A572
Chaddock La
Ullswater Road
Newlands Av
Sherwood Av
Beechwood Crs
Cranworth Av
Prince's
Norwood Av
Ley Crescent
Parkfield Avenue
Astley Hall Dr
Westgate Dr
Avondale Dr
Oakdale Dr
Chelford Drive
Hamilton Rd
Industrial Estate
A580(T)
Windsor Av
Astley St Stephens CE Primary School
Church Rd
Coach Rd
Mds Gv
Hy Av
Bllcrf Dr
MANCHESTER ROAD
Wallwork Rd
Industrial Estate
Lane
Avenue
Kermishaw Nook
Penketh Av
Merton Gv
Duke St
Manor Road
Green La
Dunmail Cl
Astley
EAST LANCASHIRE ROAD
Clegg St
St Ambrose Rd
Stephens Close
Lane
High St
Ld Dr
Drive
Moorgate Drive
Brook Drive
E Lancashire Rd
Higher
Fieldhead Av
Hawkworth
Holbeck
Crossgill
Coldalhurst Lane
Ann La
E Lanc
Ellesmere St
Higher Green
Parkdale
Primary School
1 grid square represents 500 metres

Peel Lane
Primary School
Quarry
Wicheaves Crs
Our Lady & the Lancashire Martyrs School
Hilton Lane CP School
Gibson La
Elsham Dr
Mere Fold
Prescott
Lane
Windale
Chapelfield
Bowker St
Bank
Mere Cl
East
Council
Shopping Centre
High Street
Memorial Road
Madams
Wood Road
Westwood Av
Eastwood
Wardley Av
Hilton
Aspinall Cl
Fairy
Worsley
Cartleach La
Jonquil Dr
Aspinall Crs
Avon Cl
Avenue
Weaver Av
Calder Drive
Kent Close
Trent Drive
Derwent Cl
Joseph Eastham Primary School
St Georges RC High School
Parsonage Dr
Parsonage Road
Hyde Gv
Hyde Dr
Hyde Road
Melton Cl
Charnwood Cl
Brougham St
South Gv
Tynesbank
Tyne
Campbell Wy
West Av
Council Building
Athens Dr
Bridgewater Road
B5232
Guild Av
Wilton Road
St George's Crs
Stanley Rd
Works
Brindley St
Ainsley Gv
Road
Park
Rutland Rd
Salford College
Stafford Rd
Warwick Rd
Fold Av
Edge Fold
Broadway
Bedford Av
Rochester Av
Parr
Infant & Junior School
Lansdowne Dr
Normanby Rd
Newearth Road
Endsley Av
Washbrook Avenue
Mather Fold Rd
Waverley Rd
Kinnerly Grove
Lwr New Rw
City Road
New City Rd
Ellenbrook
Hurstfield Rd
Queensway
Medway Rd
Everard Cl
Mellor Dr
Carlton Rd
Claughton Av
Harbourne Av
Ladybridge Avenue
Shawbrook Av
Lynton Crs
Duchy Av
Valdene Dr
Ellendale Gra
Ladymere Dr
Goodshaw Rd
Ladyhill Vw
Longwall Av
Reedley Dr
Ellenbrook Primary School
Greylag Crs
Doefield Av
Ellerbeck Crs
Cornlea Dr
Hindburn Dr
Bridgewater Road
Arkholme
Edenvale
Rose Acre
Oriole Dr
Oriole Cl
Ellenbrook Rd
Moor
Queen Ann Dr
Bellpit Cl
East Lancashire Road
A580(T)
Mosley Common
Common Side Road
Primary School
Worsley Business Park
School
Mosley Common
Berwick Cl
Ashdown Dr
Turncroft Wy
Tybyrne Cl
Mark St
Glendale Road
Lancashire Rd
Wyre Drive
Windlehurst Drive
Orchard Av
Wyre Dr
Birchfield Drive
Standfield Dr
Lymefield Dr
Maplefield Dr
Bankfield Dr
Stetchworth Dr
Abbot's Fold Rd
M28
Golf
Road
Ellenbrook
Clough Dr
Rands
Crosslands Rd
Mill St
School
Chaddock Lane
Boothstown
Linden Ms
Linden Road
Ashford Av
Ridgmont Drive
Brett Rd
Victoria St
Simpson Gv
Beech Av
Haydock Drive
Braemar Lane
Simpson Road
A572
Leigh Road
Sandringham Road
Booth's Hall Rd
Booth's Hall Wy
Hilton Crs
Boothsbank Avenue
Falconwood Cha
Leigh Road
Haile Dr
Brookfield Dr
Gardens
St Andrew Primary School
Grove Hl
Sterndale Rd
Hutton
Vicars Hall Lane
Boothstown Dr
Boothshall Way
Poynt Cha
Highclove
Amberhill Way
Godmond Hall
Cleabarrow Dr
Holme Pk
Vicars
E
F
G
H
I
2
3
4
5
41
72
73
02
03
401

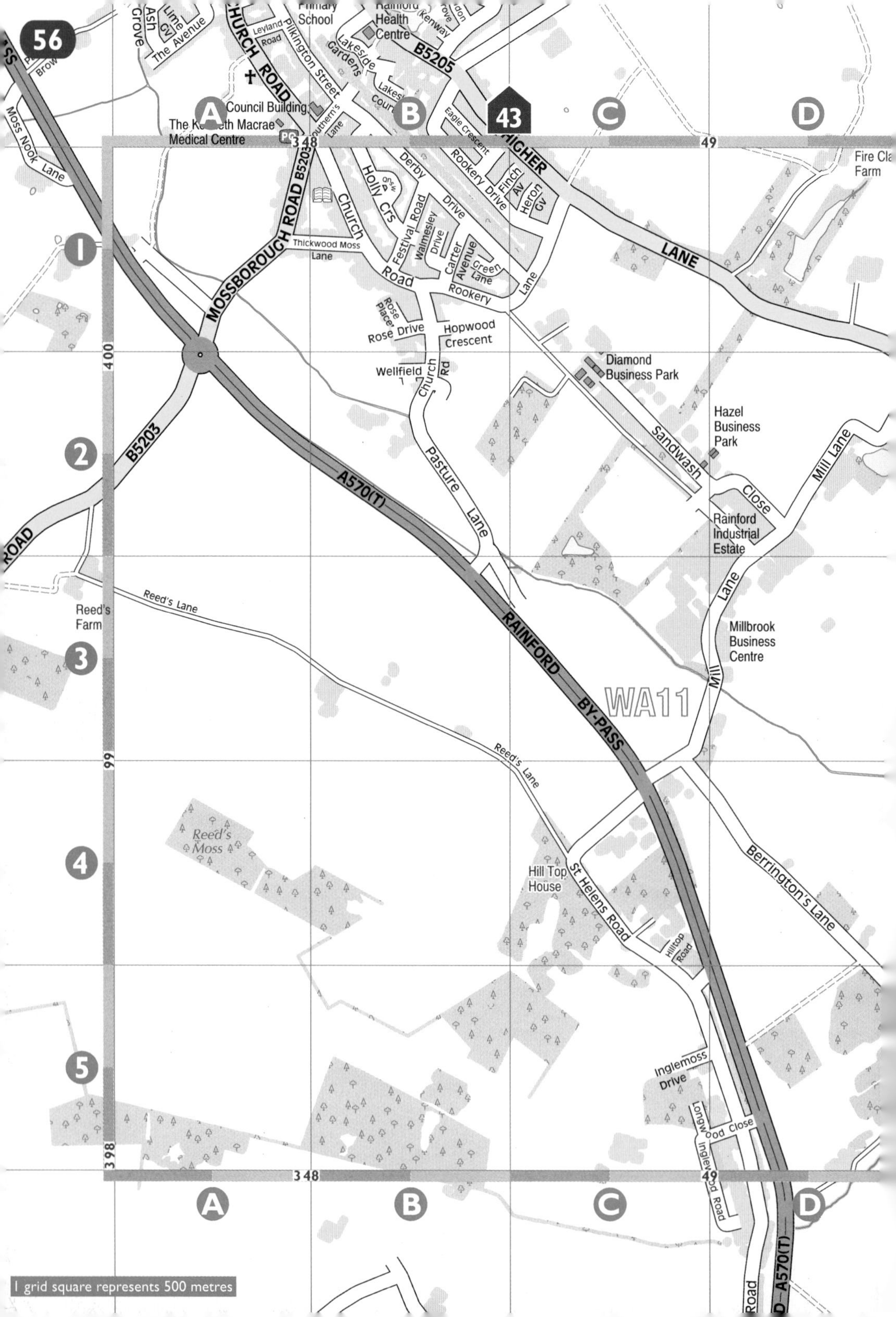
56
43
A
B
C
D
1
2
3
4
5
348
49
400
99
398
Ash Grove
Lime Gv
The Avenue
Leyland Road
Pilkington Street
Primary School
Rainford Health Centre
Kenway
Lakeside Gardens
Lakeside Court
B5205
CHURCH ROAD
Council Building
The Kenneth Macrae Medical Centre
Moss Nook Lane
Brow
Southern's Lane
Eagle Crescent
HIGHER LANE
Derby Drive
Rookery Drive
Finch Av
Heron Gv
Holly Crs
Church Road
MOSSBOROUGH ROAD B5203
Thickwood Moss Lane
Festival Road
Walmesley Drive
Carter Avenue
Green Lane
Rookery Lane
Rose Place
Rose Drive
Hopwood Crescent
Wellfield
Church Rd
Fire Clay Farm
Diamond Business Park
Hazel Business Park
Sandwash Close
Mill Lane
Rainford Industrial Estate
Millbrook Business Centre
Pasture Lane
B5203
ROAD
A570(T)
RAINFORD BY-PASS
WA11
Reed's Lane
Reed's Farm
Reed's Moss
Hill Top House
St Helens Road
Hilltop Road
Berrington's Lane
Inglemoss Drive
Longwood Close
Inglewood Road
Road
1 grid square represents 500 metres

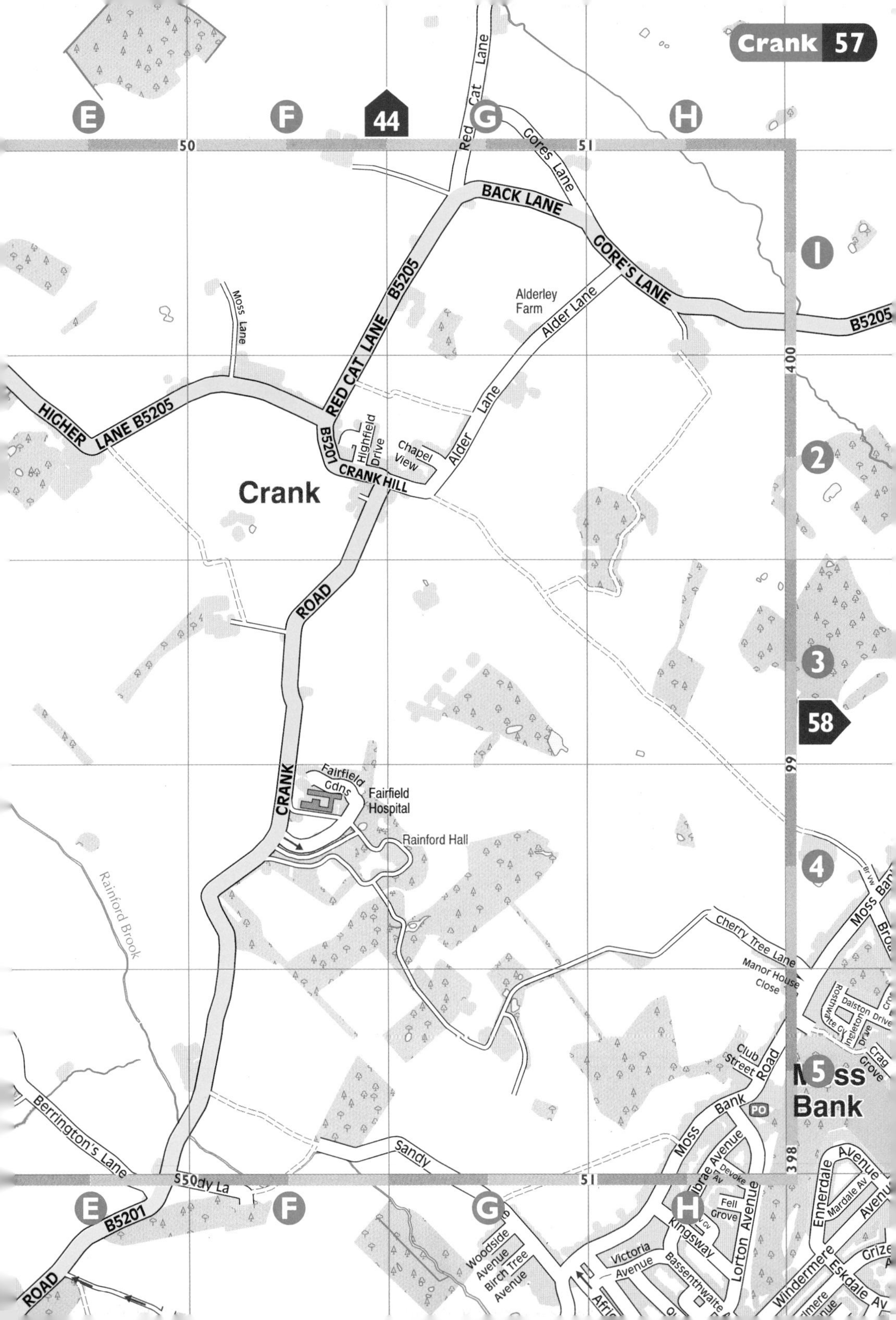

E
F
44
G
H
50
51
Red Cat Lane
Gores Lane
BACK LANE
GORE'S LANE
B5205
Moss Lane
Alderley Farm
Alder Lane
RED CAT LANE B5205
HIGHER LANE B5205
B5201
Highfield Drive
Chapel View
CRANK HILL
Crank
400
ROAD
58
99
CRANK
Fairfield Gdns
Fairfield Hospital
Rainford Hall
Rainford Brook
Cherry Tree Lane
Manor House Close
MOSS BANK
Club Street
Road
Moss Bank
PO
Berrington's Lane
Sandy
Sandy La
398
B5201
ROAD
Woodside Avenue
Birch Tree Avenue
Victoria Avenue
Kingsway
Bassenthwaite
Lorton Avenue
Fell Grove
Devoke Av
Ennerdale Avenue
Mardale Av
Windermere
Eskdale Av
Dalston Drive
Ingleton Drive
Crag Grove
1
2
3
4
5

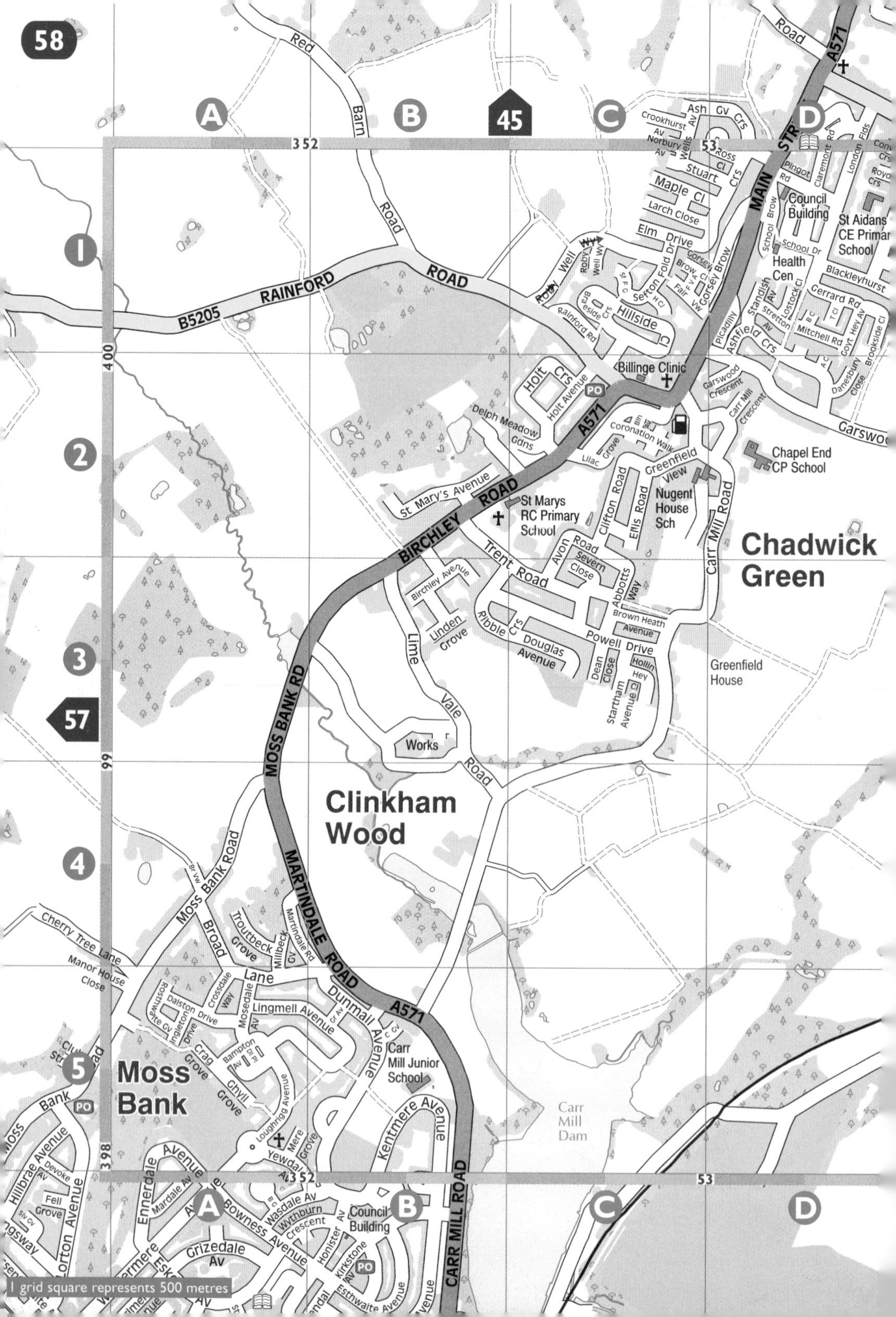
A
B
45
C
D
352
53
1
2
3
4
5
57
400
99
398
Red Barn Road
RAINFORD ROAD
B5205
MAIN STREET
A571
Ash Gv
Crs
Crookhurst Av
Norbury Av
Wells Av
Ross Cl
Stuart Crs
Maple Cl
Larch Close
Elm Drive
Roby Well Wy
Sefton Fold Dr
Gorsey Brow
Hillside Cl
Braeside Crs
Rainford Rd
Billinge Clinic
Holt Crs
Holt Avenue
PO
Delph Meadow Gdns
Coronation Walk
Lilac Grove
Greenfield View
Pingot Rd
Claremont Rd
London Flds
Royon Crs
Council Building
St Aidans CE Primary School
School Brow
School Dr
Health Cen
Blackleyhurst
Cerrard Rd
Standish Av
Lostock Cl
Stretton Av
Mitchell Rd
Goyt Hey Av
Brookside Cl
Piccadilly
Ashfield Crs
Garswood Crescent
Carr Mill Crescent
Danesbury Close
Garswood
Chapel End CP School
St Mary's Avenue
BIRCHLEY ROAD
St Marys RC Primary School
Clifton Road
Ellis Road
Nugent House Sch
Carr Mill Road
Chadwick Green
Avon Road
Severn Close
Trent Road
Abbotts Way
Birchley Avenue
Linden Grove
Ribble Crs
Douglas Avenue
Brown Heath Avenue
Powell Drive
Dean Close
Hollin Hey
Startham Avenue
Greenfield House
Lime Vale Road
Works
MOSS BANK RD
Clinkham Wood
Moss Bank Road
Br Vw
Cherry Tree Lane
Manor House Close
Broad Lane
Troutbeck Grove
Millbeck Gv
Martindale Rd
MARTINDALE ROAD
Crossdale Way
Mosedale Av
Dalston Drive
Ingleton Drive
Lingmell Avenue
Dunmail Avenue
Carr Mill Junior School
Crag Grove
Bampton Av
Chyll Grove
Moss Bank
Loughrigg Avenue
Mere Grove
Yewdale
Kentmere Avenue
Carr Mill Dam
Ennerdale Avenue
Mardale Av
Hillbrae Avenue
Devoke Av
Fell Grove
Lorton Avenue
Bowness Avenue
Wasdale Av
Wythburn Crescent
Council Building
Honister Av
Kirkstone Av
Grizedale Av
Esthwaite Avenue
CARR MILL ROAD
1 grid square represents 500 metres

Wigan
St. Helens
E
F
46
G
H
54
55
NEWTON ROAD
Windsor Road
BILLINGE
B5207
BILLINGE ROAD
Simm's Lane End
Garswood United FC
Leyland
Green Road
Downall Green
Hawthorn Av
Lilac Av
Rectory
Birch
Elm
Palm Av
Poplar Av
Cedar Gv
Grove
Blackley Hurst Hall
Road
Garswood Road
Smock Lane
Peebles Close
Thornhill Road
Stirling Drive
Selkirk Avenue
Falkland Dr
Oban Drive
Dunblane Close
Argyll Close
Girvan
Langholm Road
Hamilton
Darvel Av
Kinross Avenue
School
Forres Gv
Victoria Road
Coldstone Drive
Station Road
Manor Close
Old Colliery Yard
Surgery
PO
School Lane
Garswood Station
Works
Arch Lane
Garswood
60
Tithebarn
Garswood Old Road
Old Garswood Hall Farm
Liverpool Road
A58
LIVERPOOL ROAD
400
99
398
1
2
3
4
5

Downall Green RC Primary School
DOWNALL GREEN ROAD
Primary Sch
BRYN RD
ROAD
Surg
PO
Pasture Cl
Meadowcroft
Jennet Hey
Ferrer St
The Paddock
Kinder Gv
Sefton Road
Brockstedes Av
Coronation St
Booth's Brow Rd
A
B
C
D
47
Bryn
Bryn Stn
Clifton Rd
356
57
Green Road
Lilac Av
Rectory Road
Rectory CE Primary Sch
B5207
Hawthorn Av
Palm Av
Poplar Av
Elm Av
Everton St
Bolton St
Cedar Gv
Poplar Av
Birch Grove
Fernlea Gv
Brambles
Chantry Wk
Alder Av
Grange Road
Regent Av
Linden Av
Richmond Road
Whitledge Rd
Clough Grove
Woolton Cl
Hale Gv
Priory Road
Bevington St
Strathmore Av
Wentworth Rd
Bedford Pl
Nostell Rd
Whitledge Gn
Old Road
Wolsey Cl
Roman Rd
Surg
Bispham Dr
Ellesmere Rd
Lytham Rd
Medway Wy
Harlech St
Grantley St
Harold Av
Hardwick Rd
Frederick St
Surgery
Ashland Avenue
Clarence St
Wentworth Road
Ashton Leisure Centre
Wolmer St
Alton Close
Tatton Drive
WN4
Thornton Close
Road
PO
Cansfield Grove
Grove Street
Crescent Avenue
400
Stirling Drive
Selkirk Avenue
Peebles Close
Thornhill Road
Lane
Falkland Dr
Dunblane Close
Girvan Crs
Road
Victoria Road
Elgin Avenue
Spindle Hillock
Gordon Avenue
Austin Avenue
The Clough
Elstead Grove
Abinger Road
Hillbeck Crescent
Low Bank
Balliol Way
Wolfson Sq
Tenbury Drive
Oriel Road
Magdalen Drive
Girton Av
Greyfriars
Westfield Av
Cranbrook Av
Solway Close
Briar Close
Grey Road
Langholm Road
Darvel Av
Hamilton
Forres
School
Coldstone Drive
Hollins Close
Camp Road
Infant School
Station Road
Manor Close
Nwbr Cl
Strange Road
Salkeld Av
Lazenby Crs
Orton Way
Woodedge
Bardale Grove
Rigby Street
Surgery
PO
Berrington Grove
Calverhall Way
Dawley Close
Winchester Avenue
3
Garswood Road
Garswood Station
59
Houghwood Gra
M6
Alderton Drive
Liverpool Road
Edgerley Place
Park Industrial Estate
Gibbon's Road
Junction 24
A58
LIVERPO
99
Satinwood Close
Pinewood
Oakwood Av
Tithebarn Road
Firwood Grove
Old Hall Dr
Willowfield Gv
4
A58
LIVERPOOL ROAD
Garswood Park
Ashton-In-Makerfield Golf Club
Golf Course
Millfield Lane
5
Hall Wood Avenue
Winchester Road
Andover Road
Salisbury Road
398
68
Haydock Lane Industrial Estate
Haydock
Kilbuck Lane
Kilbuck Lane
1 grid square represents 500 metres
Bahama Close
Fishwicks Industrial
Old Boston

Stubshaw Cross
South Lancashire Industrial Estate
Ashton Grange Industrial Estate
Town Green
ASHTON-IN-MAKERFIELD
Haydock Park Racecourse
Haydock Park
Jameson's Farm
St Thomas C of E School
Prim Sch
Ashton Town AFC
School
Hotel
BOLTON ROAD A58
BOLTON ROAD
B5207
COLBORNE ROAD
WARRINGTON ROAD A49
WIGAN ROAD
GERARD STREET
BRYN STREET
LODGE LANE
Wigan St Helens
Riding Lane
Heath Road
Ashton Heath
Lincoln Drive
Princess Road
York Road
Walford Road
Hilton Street
Edward Dr
Coniston Av
Alexandra Road
Belvedere Road
Lockett Road
Haydock Park Gardens
Flora Street
Violet Street
Park View
Bransford Close
Kiveton Dr
Newlyn Drive
Tintern Avenue
Norwich Avenue
Ripon Drive
Chester Drive
Blenheim Road
Monmouth Crescent
Mill St
Chestnut Grove
White Lodge Drive
Heather Grove
Rushmoor Av
Upland Drive
Conway Rd
Severn Road
Moorland Rd
Wotton Drive
Soane Cl
Wyatt Grove
Salvin Close
Mansart Cl
Allscott Way
Dunsdale Drive
Moxon Wy
Harvey
Helen
Edge Green
E F G H
48 62 69
58 59
400 99 398
I 2 3 4 5

62
49
61
70
A
B
C
D
1
2
3
4
5
360
400
99
398
61
Riding Lane
Crankwood Road
Chadwick's Farm
Aye Bridge Farm
AYE BRIDGE ROAD
A573
Lightshaw Lane
Edge Green
Edge Green Road
Dam Lane
ASHTON ROAD
B5207
WIGAN ROAD
CHURCH STREET
LOWTON ROAD
Golborne High School
Golborne Clinic
Heywood Av
Rothwell Road
Harvey Lane
Hell Nook
Mansfield St
Helen St
Park Avenue
Halewood Av
Watson Avenue
Ringley Avenue
Gawsworth Road
Whitlow Avenue
Sycamore Av
Willow Gv
Bank Street
Barton St
Charles St
Beech Rd
St Thomas CE Primary Sch
Cottesmore Wy
Gloucester Av
Naylor Av
Oak Av
Briar Road
Tanner's Lane
Golborne CP School
John Street Medical Cen
Mill St
Manor Avenue
Windsor Rd
Derby Road
Ullswater Rd
Rivington Av
Pennine La
Pendle Rd
Sandling Dr
Millingford Av
Manley Av
Farefield Avenue
Linton Avenue
Walters Gn Crs
May St
Ash Street
Rock St
Dove St
School
Hazel Gv
Barrowdale Rd
Forster St
Duke Street
York St
Clarence St
Grimshaw St
Elm Av
Oakfield Av
Moreton Close
Trent Rd
Avon Rd
Welland Road
PO
1 grid square represents 500 metres

Crankwood
Plank Lane
Aspull Comm
Lowton Common
Park Lane
Crankwood Road
Leeds and Liverpool Canal
Horrocks Street
Cunliffe Court
Plank Lane
Mossley Hall
Byrom Hall
Byrom Lane
Green Lane
Slag Lane
Sandy Lane
Woodvale Drive
Linbeck Grove
Brook Lynn Avenue
Haddon Road
Scott Road
Ivanhoe Av
Carlton Road
Balmoral Av
Hilary Avenue
Crow Wd Rd
Waverley Rd
Marmion Cl
Ryecroft Av
Carton Drive
Beardsmore Dr
Merchants Crs
Unsworth Av
Thornbush Cl
Braithwaite Rd
Sarsfield Av
Fieldfare Cl
Surgery
The Pipers
Stone Pit Cl
Brook St
Bodden St
Pond St
Alfred Rd
Kane
Council Building
School
Industrial Estate
Barford Dr
Edgerton Rd
Clayton Av
Bainbridge Av
Chester Av
Plover
Garton
The Flash
Our ... of th... RC
50
64
71

Plank Lane
Firs Lane
Pennington
Aspull Common
The Flash
Pennington Flash Country Park
Leigh College Community Sixth Form College
Westleigh Cricket Club
Our Lady of the Rosary RC School
St Peters CE Junior School
Firsdale Industrial Estate
Moss Industrial Estate
Gilded Hollins Primary School
Lowton High School
Parsonage Retail Park
Leigh RUFC
ATHERLEIGH WAY
ST HELENS ROAD
TWIST LANE
A578
A572
A579
51
63
72
1 square represents 500 metres

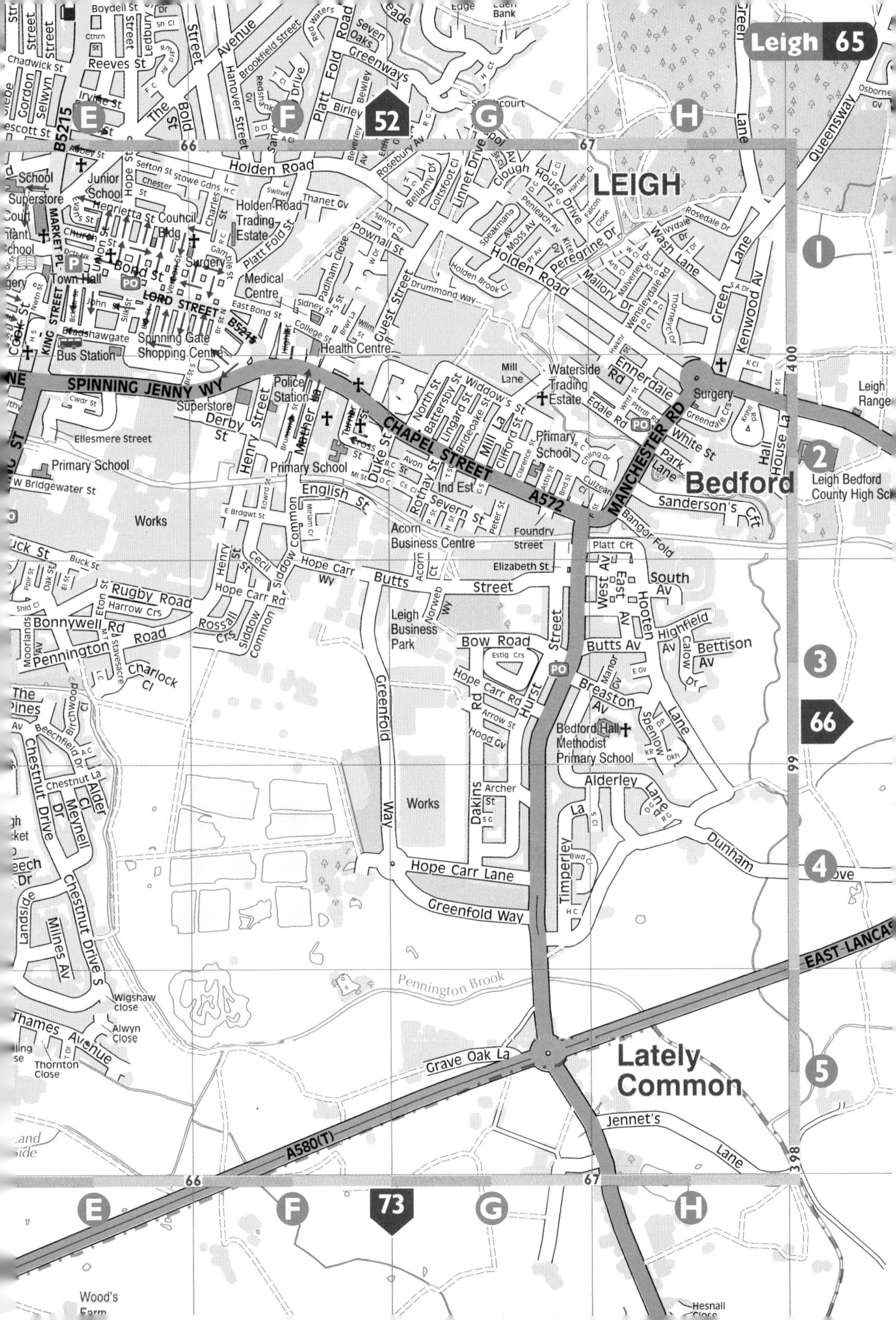
LEIGH
Bedford
Lately Common
Holden Road
Holden Road Trading Estate
Spinning Jenny Wy
Chapel Street
A572
Manchester Rd
B5215
Lord Street
King Street
Market Pl.
Bond St
Town Hall
Bus Station
Spinning Gate Shopping Centre
Council Bldg
Junior School
Superstore
Medical Centre
Health Centre
Police Station
Primary School
Surgery
Works
Acorn Business Centre
Leigh Business Park
Waterside Trading Estate
Ind Est
Foundry Street
Bedford Hall Methodist Primary School
Leigh Bedford County High Sch
Leigh Range
Butts Street
Hope Carr Lane
Greenfold Way
Hurst Street
Rugby Road
Pennington Road
Bonnywell Rd
Chestnut Drive
Chestnut Drive S
Milnes Av
Thames Avenue
Wigshaw Close
Alwyn Close
Thornton Close
Grave Oak La
A580(T)
East Lancas
Pennington Brook
Jennet's Lane
Dunham
Alderley Lane
Timperley La
Breaston Av
Butts Av
Bow Road
South Av
Hooten
Highfield Av
Bettison Av
Sanderson's Cft
Bangor Fold
Ennerdale Rd
Edale Rd
Wash Lane
Green Lane
Kenwood Av
Queensway
Hall House La
English St
Henry Street
Derby St
Duke St
Mill La
Widdow's St
Clifford St
Lingard St
Battersby St
North St
Guest Street
Pownall St
Padiham Close
Platt Fold St
Greenways
Platt Fold Road
Bold St
Hanover Street
Avenue
Reeves St
Seven Oaks
Peregrine Dr
Mallory Dr
Linnet Drive
Clough
Ellesmere Street
Buck St
Hope Carr Wy
Siddow Common
Rossall Crs
Charlock Cl
The Pines
Wood's Farm
Hesnall Close
E
F
G
H
52
66
67
73
400
399
398
1
2
3
4
5

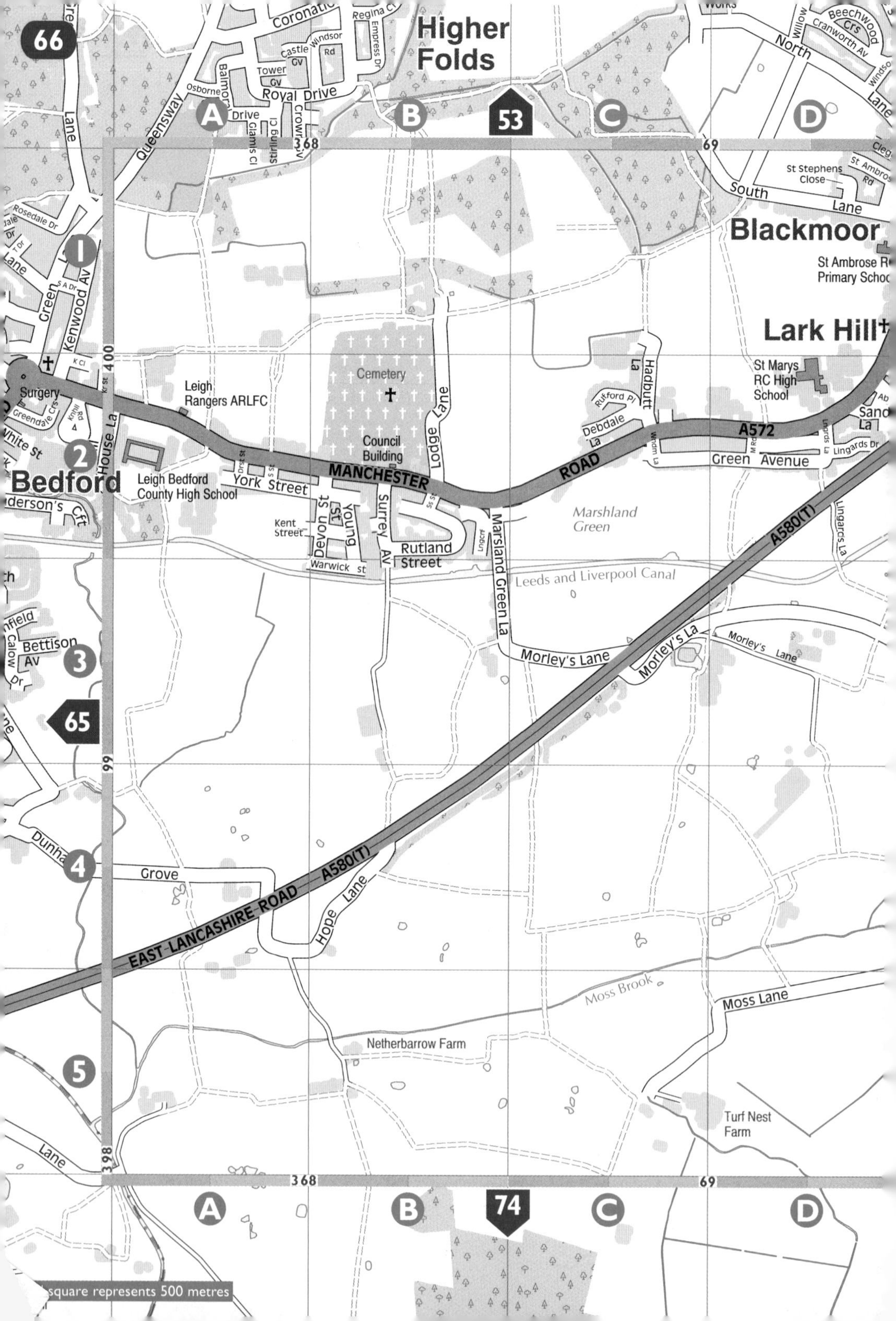

66
Higher Folds
53
Blackmoor
Lark Hill
Bedford
Manchester Road
A572
East Lancashire Road
A580(T)
Leeds and Liverpool Canal
Marshland Green
Morley's Lane
Moss Brook
Moss Lane
Netherbarrow Farm
Turf Nest Farm
Hope Lane
Grove
Cemetery
Council Building
Leigh Rangers ARLFC
Leigh Bedford County High School
St Marys RC High School
St Ambrose R
Primary Schoo
Surgery
York Street
Rutland Street
Warwick St
Devon St
Young St
Surrey Av
Lodge Lane
Marsland Green La
Hadbutt La
Debdale La
Rufford Pl
Green Avenue
Lingards Dr
Lingards La
Royal Drive
Queensway
South Lane
North Lane
St Stephens Close
Kenwood Av
Bettison Av
Calow Dr
House La
65
74
368
69
400
99
398
square represents 500 metres

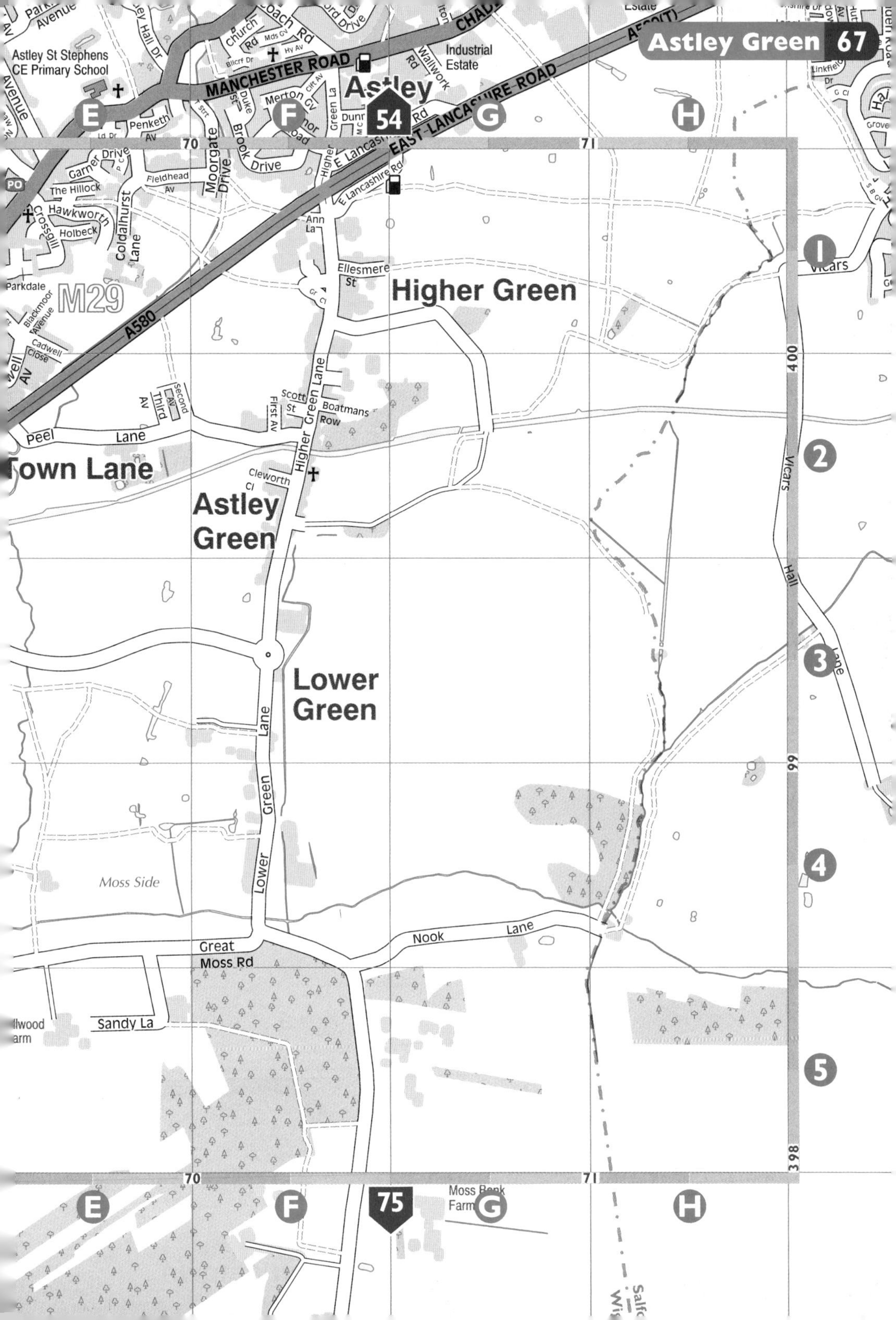
Astley St Stephens
CE Primary School
MANCHESTER ROAD
EAST LANCASHIRE ROAD
Industrial
Estate
Astley
54
Penketh
Av
Garner Drive
Fieldhead
Av
Moorgate
Drive
Brook
Drive
The Hillock
Hawkworth
Crossgill
Holbeck
Coldalhurst
Lane
Parkdale
Blackmoor
Avenue
Cadwell
Close
M29
A580
E Lancashire Rd
Ann
La
Ellesmere
St
Higher Green
Vicars
Higher Green Lane
Scott
St
Boatmans
Row
First Av
Third
Av
Second
Av
Peel
Lane
Town Lane
Cleworth
Cl
Astley
Green
Vicars
Hall
Lane
Lower
Green
Lower
Green
Lane
Moss Side
Great
Moss Rd
Nook
Lane
Sandy La
Moss Bank
Farm
75
E
F
G
H
70
71
400
399
398
1
2
3
4
5

60
A
B
C
D
1
2
3
4
5
356
57
98
97
396
HAYDOCK
New Boston
Earlestown
Haydock Lane Industrial Estate
Yew Tree Trading Estate
Fishwicks Industrial Estate
Old Boston Trading Estate
Haydock Cricket Club
Haydock Medical Centre
Primary School
St James C of E Infant School
Junior School
Grange Valley Primary School
Lyme County Infant School
The Manor CE Junior School
Central Works
Works
Council Building
Newton Common
A580(T)
EAST LANCASHIRE ROAD
A599
PENNY
CHURCH ROAD
VISTA ROAD
B5209
CROW LANE
COMMON ROAD
Haydock Lane
Hall Wood Avenue
Andover Road
Salisbury Road
Winchester Road
Kilbuck Lane
Millfield Lane
Kenyons Lane North
Kenyon's Lane South
N Florida Rd
North Florida Road
Bahama Close
Bahama Rd
Withins Road
Wycliffe Road
Elizabeth Road
Manor Road
Jubilee Crs
Beech Av
Alfred Road
James Road
Harold Road
Cook Avenue
Arrowsmith Rd
Sherlock Avenue
Pimblett Rd
Marian Rd
Piele Road
Primrose Grove
Bluebell Av
Willow Road
Birch Rd
Hall Rd
Cedar Gv
Oak Av
Woodside
Taylor Road
Aster Close
Shaftway
Westminster Dr
Fountains Av
St Albans Close
Buckfast Avenue
Coronation Drive
Princess Av
Norman Av
Queens Road
King George Road
Southward Road
Windsor Drive
Gt Delph
Chisledon Cl
Ashbury Drive
Badbury Cl
Albury Cl
Askett Cl
Dunsmore Close
Haydock Road
Woolston Rd
Woolston Road
Mercer Road
Poplar Road
Pine Cl
Station Road
Oakthorn Grove
Branch Way
Chapel Street
Chapel St
Lyme Street
Wrigley Road
Wharmby Road
Hunt Road
Shaw Street
Finney Grove
Nathan Dr
Rose Avenue
Hyacinth Cl
Moore Drive
Lupin Drive
Tulip Road
Grange Valley
Gray Avenue
Canon Wilson Cl
Heyes Av
Grange Road
Swan Road
Lyme Street
Lancaster Close
Clarence St
Brunswick Rd
Troutbeck Avenue
Birch Crs
Acacia St
Manor Av
Dene Av
Siddeley Drive
Vista Way
Rushy Vw
Heather Brae
Back Market St
Market St
Haydock St
Yew Tree Av
Cromwell
Annette Av
Sturgess St
St John St
Cooper Av
Nelson St
Crown St
Peel St
Charnock Av
Marian Av
Barnett Av
Short Close
Lloyd Crs
Legh Street
Patterdale
Regent St
Earle Cl
Brick
Bank
Lodge Med Cen
square represents 500 metres

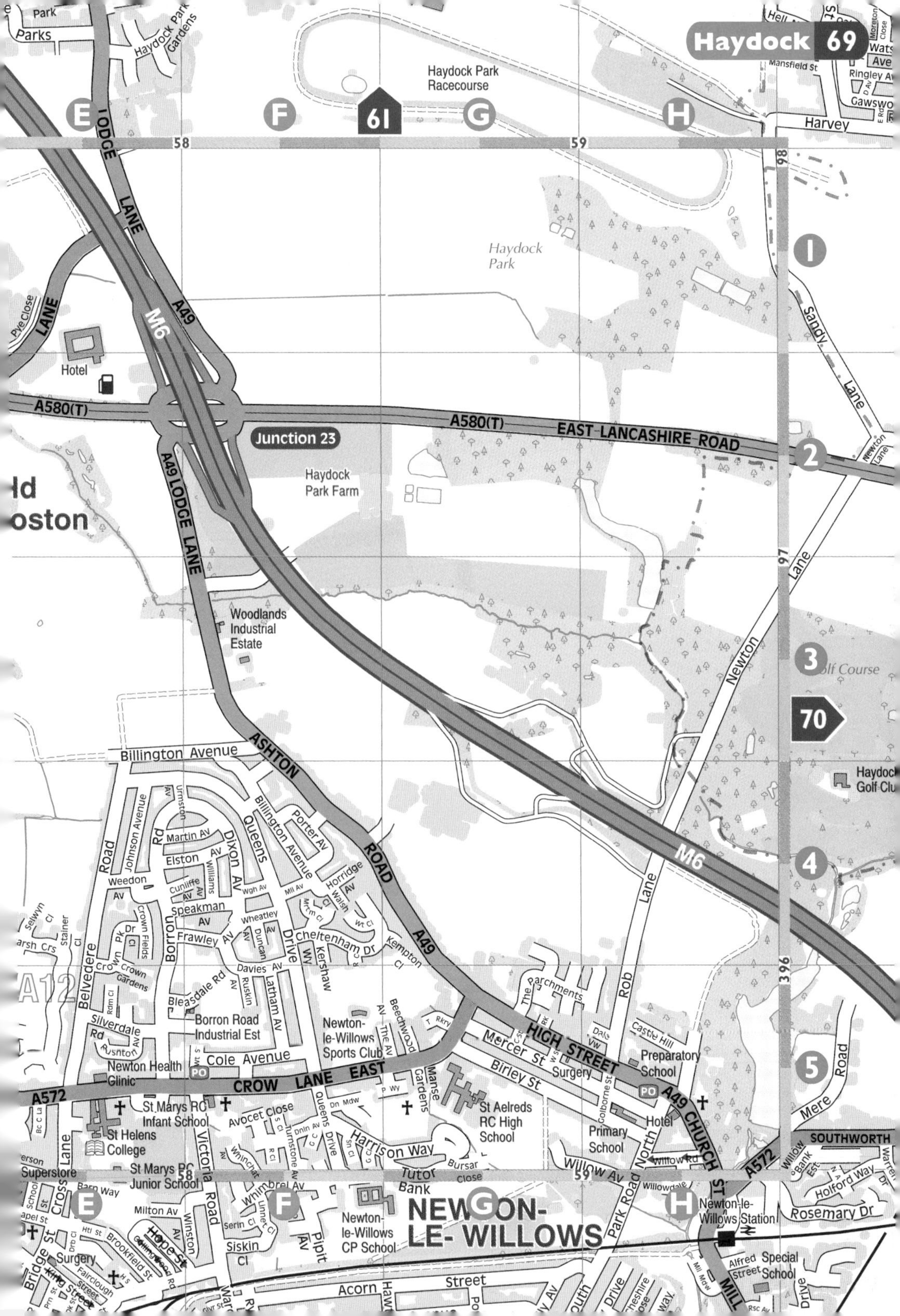
Haydock Park Racecourse
61
70
Haydock Park
Junction 23
Haydock Park Farm
A580(T)
EAST LANCASHIRE ROAD
M6
A49
A49 LODGE LANE
LODGE LANE
Hotel
Woodlands Industrial Estate
ASHTON ROAD
Billington Avenue
Sandy Lane
Newton Lane
Rob Lane
Golf Course
Haydock Golf Club
HIGH STREET
A49 CHURCH ST
A572
CROW LANE EAST
Mere Road
SOUTHWORTH
Borron Road Industrial Est
Newton Health Clinic
Newton-le-Willows Sports Club
St Aelreds RC High School
Preparatory School
Surgery
Hotel
Primary School
St Marys RC Infant School
St Helens College
St Marys RC Junior School
Superstore
Newton-le-Willows CP School
NEWTON-LE-WILLOWS
Newton-le-Willows Station
Special School
Cole Avenue
Harrison Way
Tutor Bank
Bursar Close
Willow Av
Park Road North
Victoria Road
Avocet Close
Whimbrel Av
Mercer St
Birley St
The Parchments
Castle Hill
Holford Way
Rosemary Dr
Acorn Street
Belvedere Road
Johnson Avenue
Borron Rd
Queens Drive
Kershaw Wy
Cheltenham Dr
Kempton Cl
Porter Av
Horridge Av
Latham Av
Dixon Av
Martin Av
Elston Av
Speakman Av
Frawley Av
Davies Av
Bleasdale Rd
Silverdale Rd
Crown Gardens
Weedon Av
Winston Av
Milton Av
Hope St
Brookfield St
Bridge St
King Street
Siskin Cl
Pipit Av
Cross Lane
Surgery
58
59
96
97
98
E
F
G
H
1
2
3
4
5

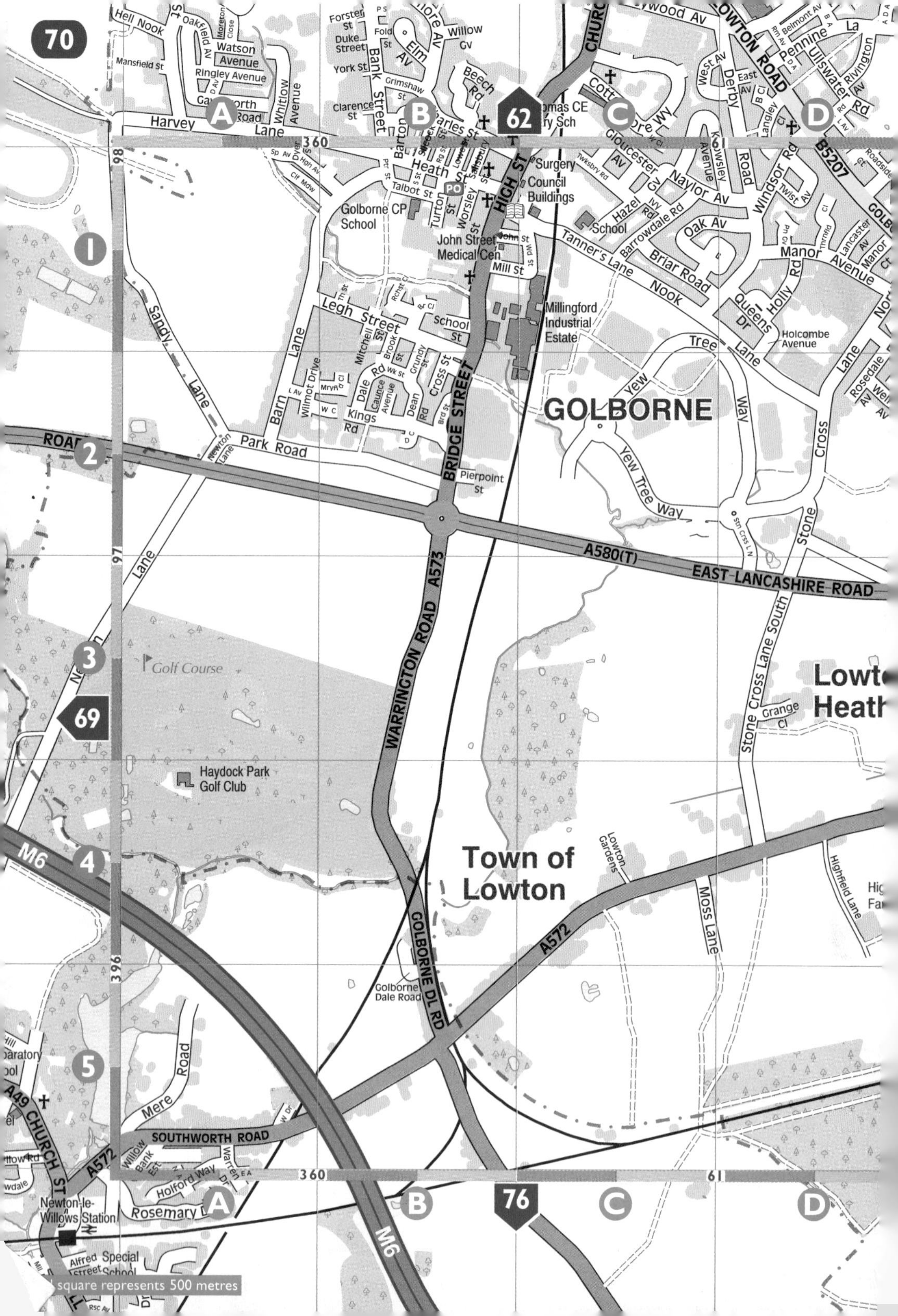

70
Hell Nook
Oakfield Av
Moreton Close
Watson Avenue
Mansfield St
Ringley Avenue
Whitlow Avenue
Harvey Lane
Forster St
Duke Street
York St
Clarence St
Bank Street
Fold St
Elm Av
Willow Gv
Grimshaw St
Beech Rd
Barton St
Charles St
Heath St
Talbot St
PO
Golborne CP School
Turton St
Worsley St
Salisbury St
HIGH ST
62
Thomas CE Primary Sch
Surgery
Council Buildings
John Street Medical Cen
John St
Mill St
Millingford Industrial Estate
Legh Street
School St
Mitchell St
Brook St
Grundy St
Cross St
Dale Rd
Wilmot Drive
Barn Lane
Kings Rd
Caunce Avenue
Dean Rd
Park Road
Sandy Lane
Newton Lane
ROAD
BRIDGE STREET
Pierpoint St
Gloucester Av
Hazel Gv
Naylor Av
Barrowdale Rd
School
Tanner's Lane
Nook Lane
Briar Road
Oak Av
Knowsley Avenue
Derby Road
East Av
West Av
LOWTON ROAD
Pennine La
Ullswater Rd
Rivington Av
Windsor Rd
Twist Av
B5207
Manor Avenue
Lancaster Av
Holly Rd
Queens Dr
Holcombe Avenue
Yew Tree Way
GOLBORNE
Rosedale Av
Cross Lane
Stone Cross Lane South
A580(T)
EAST LANCASHIRE ROAD
WARRINGTON ROAD A573
Golf Course
Haydock Park Golf Club
69
Newton Lane
Lowton Heath
Grange Cl
Town of Lowton
Lowton Gardens
Moss Lane
Highfield Lane
A572
GOLBORNE DL RD
Golborne Dale Road
M6
Mere Road
SOUTHWORTH ROAD
Willow Bank Est
Holford Way
Warren Dr
Rosemary Dr
A49 CHURCH ST
Newton-le-Willows Station
Alfred Street Special School
A B C D
1 2 3 4 5
360
98
97
396
61
76
1 square represents 500 metres

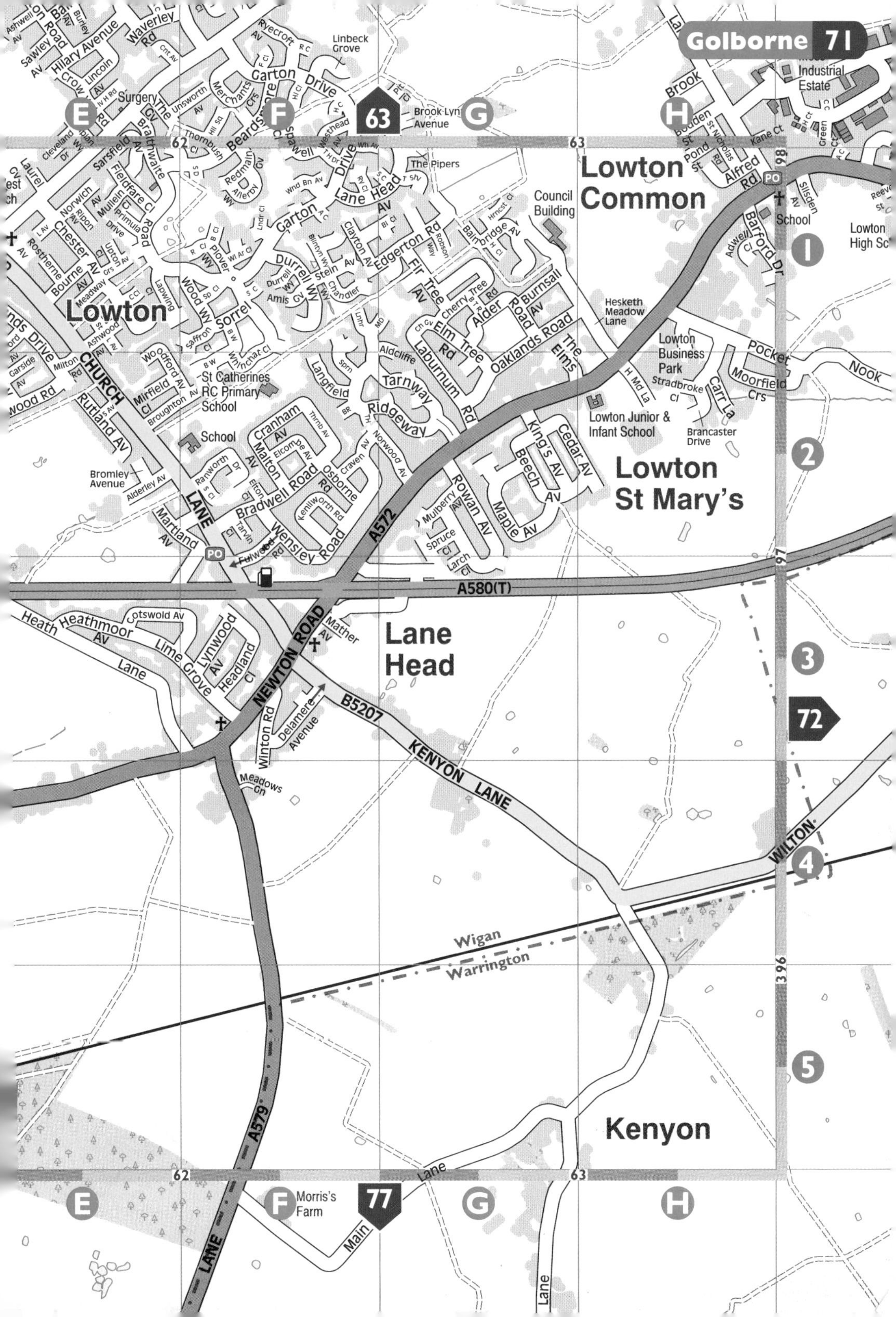
Golborne 71
Lowton
Lowton Common
Lowton St Mary's
Lane Head
Kenyon
Council Building
Surgery
Linbeck Grove
Brook Lyn Avenue
The Pipers
Industrial Estate
School
Lowton High School
Hesketh Meadow Lane
Lowton Business Park
Lowton Junior & Infant School
St Catherines RC Primary School
Bromley Avenue
Brancaster Drive
Meadows Gn
Morris's Farm
A572
A580(T)
A579
B5207
NEWTON ROAD
CHURCH LANE
KENYON LANE
WILTON
Wigan
Warrington
Heath Lane
Heathmoor Av
Cotswold Av
Lime Grove
Lynwood Av
Headland Cl
Winton Rd
Delamere Avenue
Mather Av
Wensley Road
Fulwood Rd
Martland Av
Bradwell Road
Osborne Rd
Kenilworth Rd
Cranham Av
Malton Av
Ridgeway
Tarnway
Langfield
Aldcliffe
Laburnum Rd
Elm Tree Rd
Alder Road
Oaklands Road
The Elms
Burnsall Av
Fir Tree Av
Edgerton Rd
Clayton Av
Durrell Wy
Sorrel
Garton Drive
Carton Av
Lane Head Av
Rowan Av
Maple Av
Beech Av
King's Av
Cedar Av
Mulberry Av
Spruce Cl
Larch Cl
Pocket Nook
Moorfield Crs
Carr La
Stradbroke Cl
Alfred Rd
Barford Dr
Adwell Cl
Pond St
Bouden St
Brook
Kane Ct
Slisden Av
Beardsmore Crs
Merchants
Unsworth Av
Thornbush Cl
Braithwaite Road
Sarsfield Av
Fieldfare Cl
Mullein Cl
Primula Drive
Norwich Av
Ripon Av
Chester Av
Rostherne Av
Bourne Av
Upton Av
Meadway
Ashwood Av
Milton Rd
Garside Av
Rutland Av
Alderley Av
Mirfield Cl
Woodford Av
Broughton Av
Ranworth Dr
Hilary Avenue
Crow Lincoln Av
Waverley Rd
Sawley Av
Hilary
Ryecroft Av
Carton Av
Redmain Wy
Allerby
Plover Wy
Wood Wy
Saffron Cl
Whinchat Cl
Stein Av
Chandler
Amis Gv
Cherry Tree
Bainbridge Av
Robson Way
Craven Av
Norwood Av
Elcombe Av
Elton Cl
Tarvin Cl
Lapwing
Laurel
Cleveland Dr
Main Lane
Lane
62
63
E
F
G
H
63
72
77
1
2
3
4
5
98
97
396
PO

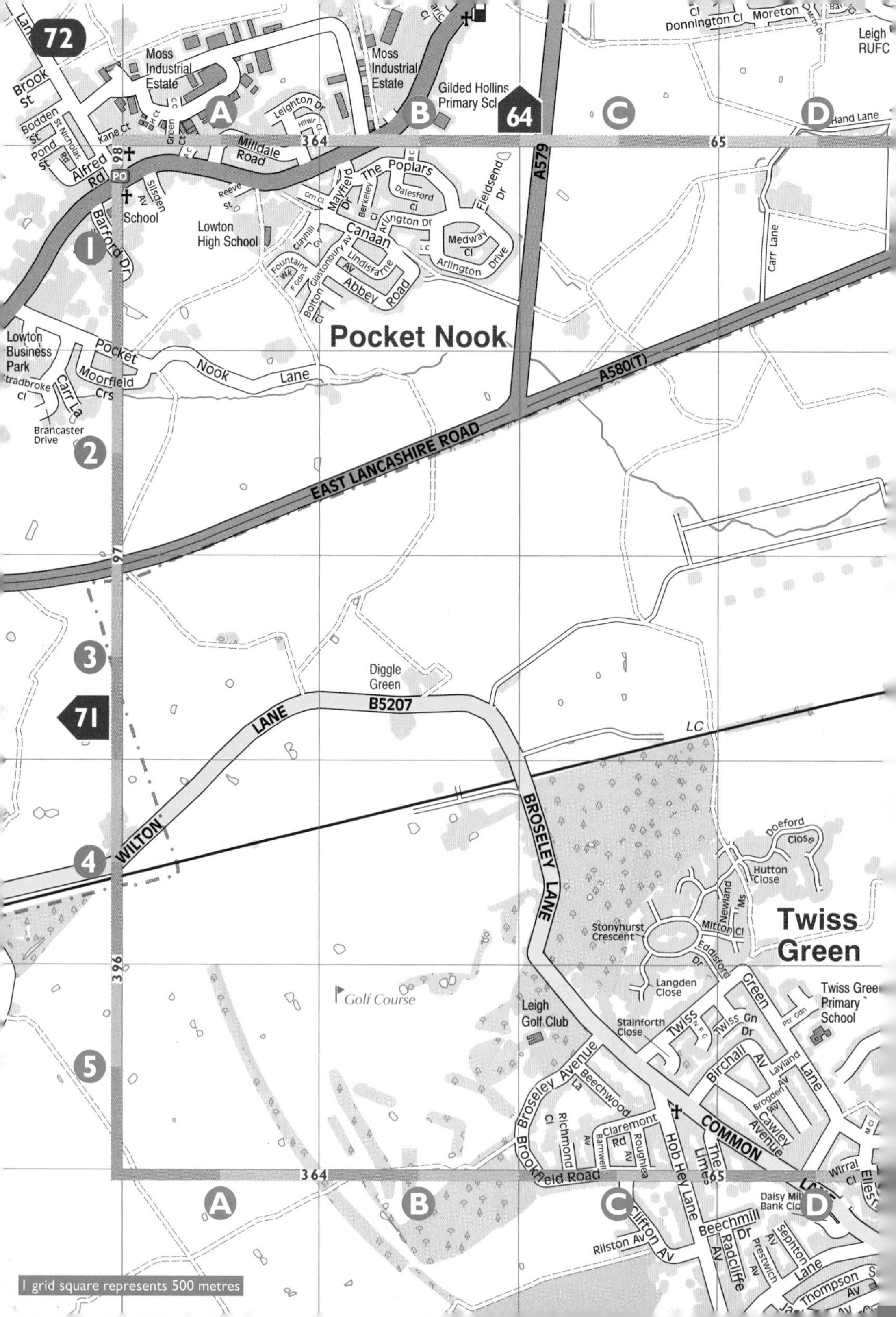

72
64
71
65
Moss Industrial Estate
Gilded Hollins Primary Sch
Donnington Cl
Moreton
Leigh RUFC
Hand Lane
Brook St
Bodden St
Pond St
St Nicholas Rd
Kane Ct
Alfred Rd
Milldale Road
Leighton Dr
Reeve St
Silsden Av
School
Lowton High School
Barford Dr
Mayfield Dr
The Poplars
Dalesford Cl
Berkeley Cl
Arlington Dr
Fieldsend Dr
A579
Medway Cl
Canaan
Claymill Gv
Glastonbury Av
Lindisfarne Av
Arlington Drive
Fountains Wk
Bolton Cl
Abbey Road
Carr Lane
Pocket Nook
Lowton Business Park
Pocket Nook Lane
Moorfield Crs
Carr La
Stradbroke Cl
Brancaster Drive
A580(T)
EAST LANCASHIRE ROAD
Diggle Green
B5207
WILTON LANE
BROSELEY LANE
LC
Doeford Close
Hutton Close
Stonyhurst Crescent
Newland Ms
Mitton Cl
Eddisford Dr
Twiss Green
Langden Close
Twiss Green Primary School
Golf Course
Leigh Golf Club
Stainforth Close
Twiss Green
Twiss Gn Dr
Birchall Av
Layland Av
Lane
Broseley Avenue
Beechwood La
Brogden Av
Cawley Avenue
Richmond Cl
Claremont Rd
Barnwell Av
Roughlea Av
COMMON
Hob Hey Lane
The Limes
Brookfield Road
Wirral Cl
Daisy Mill Bank Cl
Clifton Av
Rilston Av
Beechmill Dr
Radcliffe Av
Prestwich Av
Sephton Av
Lane
Thompson Av
A
B
C
D
1
2
3
4
5
364
396
97
98
PO
1 grid square represents 500 metres

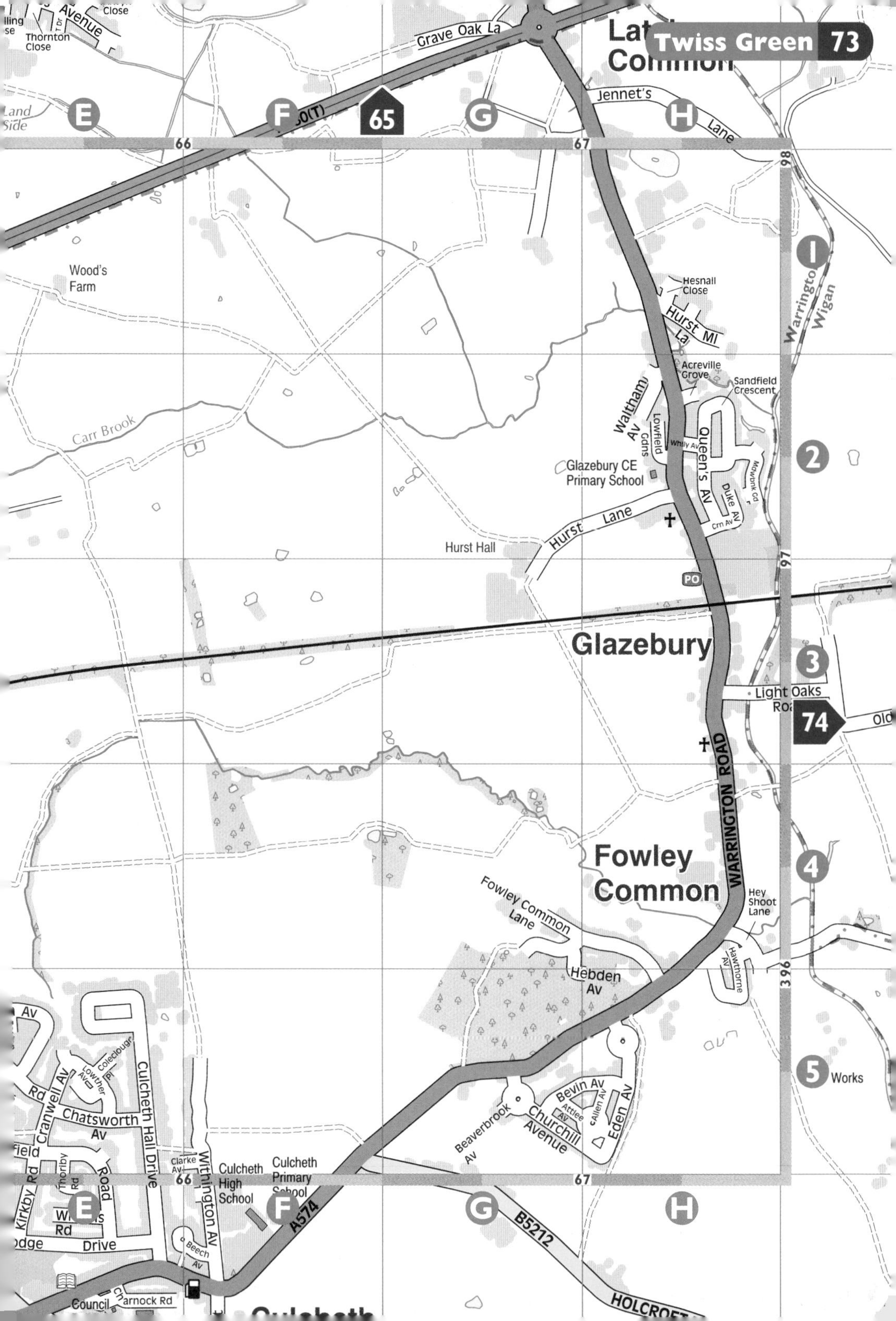
Thornton Close
Avenue
Grave Oak La
Jennet's Lane
Land Side
65
66
67
98
97
96
3
Wood's Farm
Carr Brook
Hesnall Close
Hurst Ml La
Acreville Grove
Sandfield Crescent
Waltham Av
Lowfield Gdns
Whitly Av
Queen's Av
Duke Av
Crn Av
Glazebury CE Primary School
Hurst Lane
Hurst Hall
PO
Glazebury
Light Oaks Road
74
Old
Warrington Wigan
WARRINGTON ROAD
Fowley Common
Fowley Common Lane
Hey Shoot Lane
Hawthorne Av
Hebden Av
Works
Bevin Av
Attlee Av
Allen Av
Eden Av
Churchill Avenue
Beaverbrook Av
Av
Cranwell Av
Lowther Av
Coleclough Pl
Culcheth Hall Drive
Chatsworth Av
Rd
Thornby Rd
Road
Kirkby Rd
Clarke Av
Withington Av
Culcheth High School
Culcheth Primary School
A574
B5212
Drive
Beech Av
Council
arnock Rd
HOLCROFT
E
F
G
H
I
2
3
4
5

74
Netherbarrow Farm
Turf Nest
Farm
A
B
66
C
D
Lane
368
69
98
1
Hesnall
Close
Hurst Ml
La
Warrington
Wigan
Acreville
Grove
Sandfield
Crescent
Windy Bank
Farm
Bedford
Moss
2
Whily Av
Queen's Av
Duke Av
Crn Av
PO
97
3
Light Oaks
Road
73
Old Moss Lane
Light Oaks
Moss Farm
WARRINGTON ROAD
4
Wigan
Salford
Hey
Shoot
Lane
Moss
Lane
Hawthorne
Av
396
Moss House
Farm
Holm Leigh
Farm
5
Works
368
69
A
B
C
D
1 grid square represents 500 metres

67
E
F
G
H
70
71
98
97
396
1
2
3
4
5
Moss Bank
Farm
Rindle Road
Salford
Wigan
LC
Olive Mount
Farm
Chat
Moss
Astley Road
Twelve Yards Road
Twelve Yar
Moss Farm
Raspberry La
Little
Woolden
Moss
Larkhill

76
70
A
B
C
D
Newton Park
Hermitage Green
Winwick
Newton-le-Willows Station
Special School
Red Bank School
Sankey Valley Industrial Estate
Bungalow Road
Parkside Farm
Wood Head
Red Bank
Cop Holt Farm
Warrington
St. Helens
Junction 22
Winwick CE Primary School
Winwick Parish Leisure Centre
M6
A573
A49
A572
CHURCH ST
MILL LANE
WINWICK ROAD
NEWTON ROAD
PARKSIDE ROAD
GOLBORNE ROAD
LINK ROAD
SOUTHWO ROAD
Mere Road
Rosemary Dr
Holford Way
Banastre Drive
Newton Park Drive
Wayfarers Dr
Barrow Lane
Red Bank Avenue
Hermitage Green Lane
Golborne Rd
Gerosa Av
Highfield Lane
Waterworks Lane
Old School House Lane
Green Lane
Green La Cl
The Priory
Hornby La
Myddleton Lane
Maple Rd
Ilex Av
Church Walk
Hollins Lane
Hollins Dr
Austen Dr
Arbury
Arbury Lane
Linkside Av
Course
1 grid square represents 500 metres

Kenyon
71
E
F
G
H
62
63
A579
Morris's Farm
Main Lane
WINWICK LANE
Kenyon Lane
Kenyon Hall
New Lane End
Stone Pit Lane
Sandy Brow Lane
Heath Lane
Little Town
St Lewis Primary
Oven Back Farm
95
1
2
3
4
5
Mustard Lane
Sandy La
M9A
Croft County Primary School
Wildings Old Lane
Deacon Cl
Lord St
Abbey Cl
PO
Croft
Southworth Hall Farm
Smithy Brow
Oak St
Arkenshaw Rd
Round Thorn
Betsyfield Drive
Birchall St
Gerrard Rd
Maythorn Av
Browmere Dr
Eaves Brow Rd
Pasture Dr
Eling Rd
New Lane
M6
Lane
Dam Lane
Southworth
Smithy Lane
393
Springfield Farm
Millhouse Lane

# USING THE STREET INDEX

Street names are listed alphabetically. Each street name is followed by its postal town or area locality, the Postcode District, the page number, and the reference to the square in which the name is found.

Standard index entries are shown as follows:

**Abbey Cl** *GOL/RIS/CU* WA3 .................**77** H4

Street names and selected addresses not shown on the map due to scale restrictions are shown in the index with an asterisk or with the name of an adjoining road in brackets:

**Acresfield Cl** *HOR/BR* * BL6...................**7** H4

**Albion Pk**
*GOL/RIS/CU*
(off Warrington Rd) WA3 ....................**73** H3

# GENERAL ABBREVIATIONS

ACC ACCESS
ALY ALLEY
AP APPROACH
AR ARCADE
ASS ASSOCIATION
AV AVENUE
BCH BEACH
BLDS BUILDINGS
BND BEND
BNK BANK
BR BRIDGE
BRK BROOK
BTM BOTTOM
BUS BUSINESS
BVD BOULEVARD
BY BYPASS
CATH CATHEDRAL
CEM CEMETERY
CEN CENTRE
CFT CROFT
CH CHURCH
CHA CHASE
CHYD CHURCHYARD
CIR CIRCLE
CIRC CIRCUS
CL CLOSE
CLFS CLIFFS
CMP CAMP
CNR CORNER
CO COUNTY
COLL COLLEGE
COM COMMON
COMM COMMISSION
CON CONVENT
COT COTTAGE
COTS COTTAGES
CP CAPE
CPS COPSE
CR CREEK
CREM CREMATORIUM
CRS CRESCENT
CSWY CAUSEWAY
CT COURT
CTRL CENTRAL
CTS COURTS
CTYD COURTYARD
CUTT CUTTINGS
CV COVE
CYN CANYON
DEPT DEPARTMENT
DL DALE
DM DAM
DR DRIVE
DRO DROVE
DRY DRIVEWAY
DWGS DWELLINGS
E EAST
EMB EMBANKMENT
EMBY EMBASSY
ESP ESPLANADE
EST ESTATE
EX EXCHANGE
EXPY EXPRESSWAY
EXT EXTENSION
F/O FLYOVER
FC FOOTBALL CLUB
FK FORK
FLD FIELD
FLDS FIELDS
FLS FALLS
FLS FLATS
FM FARM
FT FORT
FWY FREEWAY
FY FERRY
GA GATE
GAL GALLERY
GDN GARDEN
GDNS GARDENS
GLD GLADE
GLN GLEN
GN GREEN
GND GROUND
GRA GRANGE
GRG GARAGE
GT GREAT
GTWY GATEWAY
GV GROVE
HGR HIGHER
HL HILL
HLS HILLS
HO HOUSE
HOL HOLLOW
HOSP HOSPITAL
HRB HARBOUR
HTH HEATH
HTS HEIGHTS
HVN HAVEN
HWY HIGHWAY
IMP IMPERIAL
IN INLET
IND EST INDUSTRIAL ESTATE
INF INFIRMARY
INFO INFORMATION
INT INTERCHANGE
IS ISLAND
JCT JUNCTION
JTY JETTY
KG KING
KNL KNOLL
L LAKE
LA LANE
LDG LODGE
LGT LIGHT
LK LOCK
LKS LAKES
LNDG LANDING
LTL LITTLE
LWR LOWER
MAG MAGISTRATE
MAN MANSIONS
MD MEAD
MDW MEADOWS
MEM MEMORIAL
MKT MARKET
MKTS MARKETS
ML MALL
ML MILL
MNR MANOR
MS MEWS
MSN MISSION
MT MOUNT
MTN MOUNTAIN
MTS MOUNTAINS
MUS MUSEUM
MWY MOTORWAY
N NORTH
NE NORTH EAST
NW NORTH WEST
O/P OVERPASS
OFF OFFICE
ORCH ORCHARD
OV OVAL
PAL PALACE

PAS PASSAGE
PAV PAVILION
PDE PARADE
PH PUBLIC HOUSE
PK PARK
PKWY PARKWAY
PL PLACE
PLN PLAIN
PLNS PLAINS
PLZ PLAZA
POL POLICE STATION
PR PRINCE
PREC PRECINCT
PREP PREPARATORY
PRIM PRIMARY
PROM PROMENADE
PRS PRINCESS
PRT PORT
PT POINT
PTH PATH
PZ PIAZZA
QD QUADRANT
QU QUEEN
QY QUAY
R RIVER
RBT ROUNDABOUT
RD ROAD
RDG RIDGE
REP REPUBLIC
RES RESERVOIR
RFC RUGBY FOOTBALL CLUB
RI RISE
RP RAMP
RW ROW
S SOUTH
SCH SCHOOL
SE SOUTH EAST
SER SERVICE AREA
SH SHORE
SHOP SHOPPING
SKWY SKYWAY
SMT SUMMIT
SOC SOCIETY
SP SPUR
SPR SPRING
SQ SQUARE
ST STREET
STN STATION
STR STREAM
STRD STRAND
SW SOUTH WEST
TDG TRADING
TER TERRACE
THWY THROUGHWAY
TNL TUNNEL
TOLL TOLLWAY
TPK TURNPIKE
TR TRACK
TRL TRAIL
TWR TOWER
U/P UNDERPASS
UNI UNIVERSITY
UPR UPPER
V VALE
VA VALLEY
VIAD VIADUCT
VIL VILLA
VIS VISTA
VLG VILLAGE
VLS VILLAS
VW VIEW
W WEST
WD WOOD
WHF WHARF
WK WALK
WKS WALKS
WLS WELLS
WY WAY
YD YARD
YHA YOUTH HOSTEL

## POSTCODE TOWNS AND AREA ABBREVIATIONS

AIMK Ashton-in-Makerfield
ATH Atherton
BOL Bolton
BOLE Bolton east
BOLS/LL Bolton south/Little Lever
BRSC Burscough
CHLY/EC Chorley/Eccleston
CHLYE Chorley east/Ardlington/Whittle-le-Woods
FWTH Farnworth
GOL/RIS/CUL Golborne/Risley/Culcheth
IRL Irlam
LEIGH Leigh
LHULT Little Hulton
NEWLW Newton-le-Willows
ORM Ormskirk
RNFD/HAY Rainford/Haydock
SKEL Skelmersdale
TYLD Tyldesley
WALK Walkden
WARRN/WOL Warrington north/Woolston
WGN Wigan
WGNE/HIN Wigan east/Hindley
WGNNW/ST Wigan northwest/Standish
WGNS/IIMK Wigan south/Ince-in-Makerfield
WGNW/BIL/OR Wigan west/Billinge/Orrell
WHTN Westhoughton

## Index - streets

## B

## D

## E



## F

## G

# H

## I



## J

# K



# L

## M

## N

## S

## T



## U

## V



## W

## Y



# Index - featured places

**Notes**

## Notes

# Notes

# Notes

# Notes

# QUESTIONNAIRE

**Dear Atlas User**
**Your comments, opinions and recommendations are very important to us. So please help us to improve our street atlases by taking a few minutes to complete this simple questionnaire.**

You do NOT need a stamp (unless posted outside the UK). If you do not want to remove this page from your street atlas, then photocopy it or write your answers on a plain sheet of paper.

**Send to: The Editor, AA Street by Street, FREEPOST SCE 4598, Basingstoke RG21 4GY**

## ABOUT THE ATLAS...

**Which city/town/county did you buy?**

______________________________

**Are there any features of the atlas or mapping that you find particularly useful?**

______________________________

______________________________

______________________________

**Is there anything we could have done better?**

______________________________

______________________________

______________________________

**Why did you choose an AA Street by Street atlas?**

______________________________

______________________________

______________________________

**Did it meet your expectations?**

**Exceeded** ☐ **Met all** ☐ **Met most** ☐ **Fell below** ☐

Please give your reasons

______________________________

______________________________

______________________________

______________________________

______________________________

*continued overleaf*

**Where did you buy it?**

---

**For what purpose?** (please tick all applicable)

**To use in your own local area** ☐ **To use on business or at work** ☐

**Visiting a strange place** ☐ **In the car** ☐ **On foot** ☐

**Other** (please state)

---

## LOCAL KNOWLEDGE...

**Local knowledge is invaluable. Whilst every attempt has been made to make the information contained in this atlas as accurate as possible, should you notice any inaccuracies, please detail them below (if necessary, use a blank piece of paper) or e-mail us at *streetbystreet@theAA.com***

---

## ABOUT YOU...

**Name (Mr/Mrs/Ms)**

**Address**

**Postcode**

**Daytime tel no**

**E-mail address**

**Which age group are you in?**

**Under 25** ☐ **25-34** ☐ **35-44** ☐ **45-54** ☐ **55-64** ☐ **65+** ☐

**Are you an AA member?** **YES** ☐ **NO** ☐

**Do you have Internet access?** **YES** ☐ **NO** ☐

---

Thank you for taking the time to complete this questionnaire. Please send it to us as soon as possible, and remember, you do not need a stamp (unless posted outside the UK).



ML